BUSINESS ENVIRONMENT

Dr.B.Hiriyappa,Ph.D.,
Assistant Professor
Sambhram Academy of Management Studies
Bangalore

Preface

Business environment is the study of business and its environment and its components. Business environment consists of internal environment and external environment. Internal environment is controllable and external environment is uncontrollable to an enterprise. External environment is divided into micro environment and macro environment. Business manager should aware of the Business environment than only he or she effectively sell products and services which offered by an enterprise to ultimate customers.

Dr.B.Hiriyappa, Ph.D.,
E-mail:drbhiriyappa@gmail.com

Chapter 1: Business Environment

- ❖ Introduction
- ❖ Definition of business
- ❖ Characteristics of business
- ❖ Components of business
- ❖ Industry
- ❖ Types of industry
- ❖ Objectives of a business
- ❖ Long term objectives of a business
- ❖ Characteristics of business environment
- ❖ Environmental influences on business
- ❖ Environmental analysis
- ❖ Environment influence on SWOT
- ❖ Components of business environment
- ❖ Relationship between organisation and its environment
- ❖ Internal analysis of the organisation / company
- ❖ The value of systematic internal assessment
- ❖ Identification of strategic factors
- ❖ Functional approach
- ❖ The value chain approach
- ❖ Identifying support activities
- ❖ Using value chain in internal analysis
- ❖ Evolution of strategic internal factors
- ❖ Stages in product / market evolution or product life cycle
- ❖ Quantitative versus qualitative approaches in evaluating internal factors of the organisation
- ❖ External environment
- ❖ Micro / operating environment
- ❖ Macro / remote environment
- ❖ Economic environment
- ❖ Political environment
- ❖ Legal environment
- ❖ Socio-cultural environment
- ❖ Demographic environment
- ❖ Natural environment
- ❖ Physical and technological environment
- ❖ Technological environment
- ❖ Global or international environment
- ❖ Strategic response to the environment
- ❖ Competitive environment

❖ Competitive advantage
❖ Five force model

CHAPTER 1
BUSINESS ENVIRONMENT

Contents

❖ Introduction
❖ Business
❖ Objectives of business
❖ Environmental influences on business
❖ Environmental analysis
❖ Characteristics of business environment
❖ Components of business environment
❖ The micro and macro environment
❖ Competitive environment
❖ Porter's Five Forces Model – competitive analysis

Learning objectives

The present chapter aims at:
- Providing the business and objective of business
- we shall examine environment analysis, characteristics components of the organization. Let us know the microenvironment and macro environment
- understand the competitive environment
- Describe the Porter's Five-Force Model and its Limitations.

"Environment factors of constraints are largely if not totally external and beyond the control of individual industrial enterprises and their arrangements. These are essentially the 'givers' within which firms and their managements must operate in a specific country and they vary , often greatly from country to country".

Barry M. Richman and Melvyn Copen

" The environment includes outside the firm which can lead to opportunities for or threats to the firm. Although, there are many factors , the most important of the sectors are soci – economic , technical , supplier , competitors , and government".

Glueck and Jauch

"Analysis is the critical starting point of strategic thinking"

Kenichi Ohmae

"It is not the strongest of the species that survive, nor the most intelligent, but the one most responsive to change".

Charles Darwin

"Strategy is a deliberate search for a plan of action that will develop a business's competitive advantage and compound it".

Bruce D. Henderson

"Awareness of the environment is not special project to be undertaken only when warning of change becomes deafening".

Clifton Garvin, Kenneth R. Andrews

INTRODUCTION

In this book, we shall discuss about the business, major objectives of business like survival, stability, growth, efficiency and profitability, environmental influence to business, environment analysis, characteristics of business environment ,components of business environment, to know the relationship between the organization and its environment, the micro and macro environment and its elements like customers , competitors , organization, market , suppliers, intermediaries, demographic , economic , government, legal, political , cultural , technological and global environment impact on business. Companies how to enter into global market, its manifestation trends, strategic response to business , Porter's competitive and five forces model analysis for business enterprises in industry, commerce and services sector.

DEFINITION OF BUSINESS

The term 'typically` refers to the development and processing of economic values in society. Normally, the term is applied to portion of economic activities whose primary purpose is to provide goods and services for society in an effective manner. It is also applied to economics and commercial activities of institutions which having other purposes.

Business principally comprises of an all profit seeking activities of the organization which provide goods and services that are necessary to economic system. It is the major economic pulse of a nation, striving to increase society's standard of living. Finally, profits are a primary mechanism for motivating these activities.

Business is in any organization which makes distribution or provides any article or service to the customers, who are belonging to members of the society. Business may be satisfied customers needs for these purpose customers are able and willing to pay for it.

Business may be defined as "the organized effort by individuals to produce goods and services to sell these goods and services in a market place and to reap some reward for this effort."

Functionally, we may define business as "those human activities which involves production or purchase of goods with the object of selling them at a profit margin"

❖ The term business refers to the state of being busy for an individual , group , organization or society.

- ❖ It is also interpreted as one's regular occupation or profession or economic activities.
- ❖ It deals with particular entity, company, organization, enterprise, firms or corporation.
- ❖ It also interpreted as particular market segment sector like computer business and it included under term business.
- ❖ It is wide and willing to use different activities
- ❖ It consists of purchase, sale, manufacture, processing , marketing of products, services like manufacturing , trading , transportation, warehousing , banking and finance, insurance and advertising etc.
- ❖ It is clearly stated that all business activities main purpose is to earn profit. Profit as a surplus of business and It accrues and distributed to the owners of the business. Business has to pay wages to workers who works in the business. People invests money in business due to getting a retain. Retain is profit from the business. This is awarded to investor because of they are taking the risk.
- ❖ Profit is the motive for the investor who serves and run business and it is the stimulation effort of the business for growth, survival of business.

Profit Is A Main Motive Of Business

- ❖ For every kind of business organization, profit is often regarded as motive for the entrepreneurs and it measure the overall performance of the business.
- ❖ Profit is the tool for measuring and evaluation of the business efficiency and productivity at the managerial competence.
- ❖ It is helpful to strategic managers how to take well decisions and actions which are turn into effective in the form of able to combine and utilize the available resource and able to sustain the organization with growth and survival of the business entity.
- ❖ Business managers who will take higher efficiency and risk and certainly expect greater volume of the profit from the business entity.
- ❖ Business efficiency expressed in terms of percentage of profit to sales volume, to capital employed , to market value of corporate shares.
- ❖ Outside investors eager to know the profit of the firm and to make assessment about their commit funds and effective utilization of funds will be in the business entity.

Business According to Prof. R. N. Owens

"Business is an enterprise engaged in the production and distribution of goods for sale in a market or rendering of services for a price".

Business According to L.R. Dicksee

"Business is a form of activity pursued primarily with the object of earning profits for the benefit of those on whose behalf the activity is conducted".

Business According to Urwick and Hunt

"Business is any enterprise which makes, distributes or provides any article or service which other members of the community need and are willing to pay for"

Business According to **Haney**

"Business may be defined as human activity directed towards producing or acquiring wealth through buying and selling of goods".

Peter F Drucker has drawn some conclusions about what is a business and what are useful from the business and how to understand the term business. His conclusions are listed below:

❖ Business is created and managed by the people A group of people who will be taken decisions that will be determined whether an organization is going to prosper or decline, whether it will survive or will eventually perish. This conclusion is true in the business.

❖ Business cannot explained in terms of profit.

CHARACTERISTICS OF BUSINESS

❖ Business is to provide goods and service to the people. It provides the public with the things it needs and wants in order to survive, enjoy life and improve in a material sense. From the point of view of consumer, business is the satisfier of needs and desire of the customer demands which should be provided by business.

❖ Goods that have been produced or procured for sale in retain for price enter the realm of business. This activity of selling results is the creation of the wealth for the society. In satisfying demand, business uses the resources of land, labor and capital. These resources when taken separately have little value; but business combines structures and refines the resources to produce to the value of the society. Further, business employees' people who exchange their talents for wages and salaries. Therefore, these people exchange their compensation for the desired goods and service.

❖ Business is profit -seeking activity. It supplies goods and services to customers who are satisfy their demand and desire. It adds to society's value by earning of a profit. Profit is the biggest stimulus for maintains the survival of the business and its future development. Society has permits business to earn profit as a reward for assuming the risks of operating a business.

❖ Business is also an essential participant in society. For satisfying society demand which supplying goods and services and earning profits.

Business involves the most fundamental activities of the society. As a result, Society has looks to business for something more than products, services and profits. It looks to business for leadership and direction in helping to achieve society's objectives. It expects business to assist in the establishment of a better service to the society.

COMPONENTS OF BUSINESS

Business includes the total enterprise of the country. Business activity has two branches. They are as follows:

- Industry
- Commerce

INDUSTRY

In broad sense, industry is the branch of business activity which concerned with raising production, fabrication or possessing of goods and services. In other words, industry is an activity concerned with conversion of raw materials or semi finished goods into finished goods. Industry provides two types of goods namely Consumer goods and Industrial goods. Consumer goods are those goods manufactured by industry for ultimate use of a customer. For instance brush, Paste, cloth and food products etc., Industrial\Capital goods are those goods produced and used for further production. For instance machineries, tools and raw material etc.,

TYPES OF INDUSTRY

Industry is further classified into five broad types. They are as listed below:

1. Extractice industries
2. Genetic industries
3. Manufacturing industries
4. Construction industries
5. Territory \ Service industries

Extractive Industry

Extractive industry are those industries concerned with extraction of wealth from surface of the earth, soil, forest, water, air etc, for instance agriculture, mining etc.,

Genetic Industries

Genetic industries are those industries concerned with reproduction and multiplication of plants animals for making profit on their sale. For example, Nurseries, cattle building and poultry farming.

Manufacturing Industries

Manufacturing industries are engaged in the conversation and process of raw material through separation, combination, and transformation into finished goods. Such as machinery and plants of all types, iron and steel, sugar, paper, cotton clothe, electrical appliances, zinc ore, paper pulp water power, etc.,

Construction Industries

Construction industries are concerned with the construction of roads, railways, dams, canals, buildings, bridges etc. there are mainly concerned with the manufacture of non-moveable items.

Territory or Service Industries

Service industry which produce intangible goods those which cannot be seen or touched included in this category are banking, transport, insurance, communication and services of a professional nature such as lawyers, doctors, dentists, management consultants, advertisers, chartered accountants and engineers, etc.,

Commerce

Commerce has been defined as "the sum total of those processes which are engaged in the removal of the hindrance of persons (trade), Place (transport and insurance), and time (warehousing) in the exchange (banking) of commodities".

Trade

Trade means sale, transfer, or exchange of goods and services, through certain ancillary functions like packing, warehousing, banking, transportation, Insurance, and advertising.

Trade may be
- Domestic Trade
- International Trade

OBJECTIVES OF A BUSINESS

Business Purpose

Business have some purpose. These purpose are listed below:

❖ It is to create customers
❖ It is create customers for selling of their products and services.
❖ It is create market.
❖ Customers determine the main purpose of the business.
❖ Customers is the basic foundation of the business and keeps its in existence in the market.
❖ It is exists because of catering to material needs and requirement of the society, individual persons, government institutions, company , firms and enterprise.
❖ Business is run with in the purview of the legal and general public interest.
❖ It is ultimate force of an economic expansion, growth and change.

In general sense, enterprise pursue multiple objectives rather than a one objectives. Strategic manager has identify a set of main business objectives . these pursued by a large cross – section of enterprises .Profitability , productivity , efficiency , growth , technological, dynamism, stability, self reliance , survival, competitive strength, customer services , financial solvency, product quality, diversification , employee satisfaction and welfare and so on are the major objectives of enterprise. Enterprise look for balance of these objectives in appropriate and suitable manner. An important business objectives are listed below:

Figure – 1.1 : Important Objectives of Business

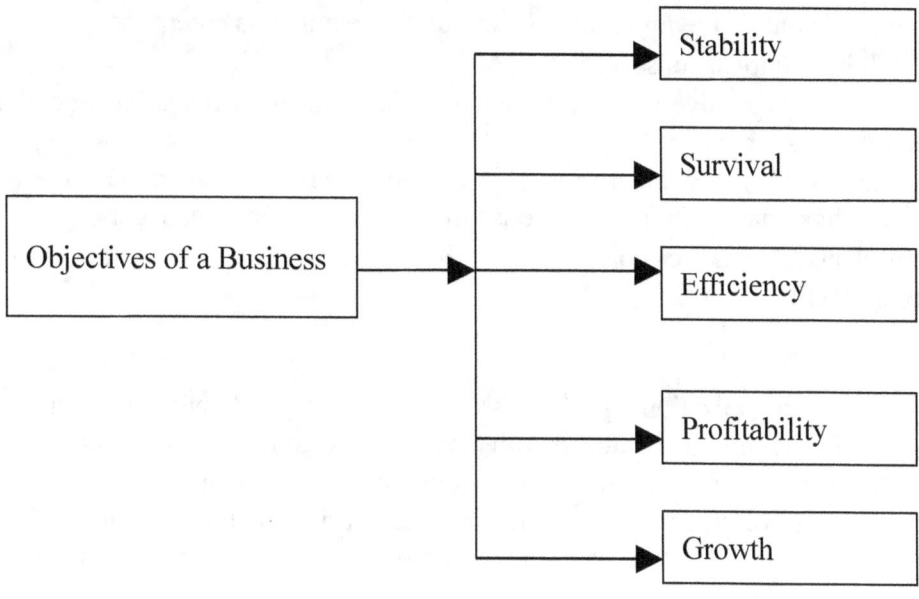

Figure 1.1 has identified the important objectives of business as outlined:
- ❖ Survival
- ❖ Stability
- ❖ Growth
- ❖ Profitability
- ❖ Efficiency

Survival

- ❖ An organization mission statement reveals the organization's intention to secure its survival through development growth and profitability of the business.
- ❖ It is will and continue the business concern into the future as long as possible perpetuate anxiety Strategic managers take more responsibility for survival of the organization business.
- ❖ Therefore, Survival is an assumed goal of the business, if strategic managers often neglected survival, its impact on strategic decisions making for long term.
- ❖ It is basic and implied objectives of the most organizations.
- ❖ It will be gained more value and important during the stage of the beginning of the business enterprise and during the general economic adversity of business.

- ❖ The survival refers to the function of the nature of ownership, nature of business competence of management, general and industry conditions, financial strength of the business enterprise or any type of business concern.
- ❖ All types of enterprises will be interested in more than mere survival.

Stability

- ❖ Stability is one of the important objectives of the business enterprise.
- ❖ It will be cautious, conservative objective
- ❖ It is a least expensive and risky objectives in form of managerial time and talent and other resources,
- ❖ A good and steady enterprise always minimizes its managerial tensions and reduces its dynamic nature decisions which are taken from managers.
- ❖ It is least resistance compare to other objectives and hostile to external environment.

Growth

- ❖ An organization growth is closely associated with its survival and profitability and equated with dynamism, vigour , promise , and success.
- ❖ Growth refers to overall development of the organization activities in terms of increase in assets , manufacturing facilities , increase in sales volume in existing or through new product in this way improve profits and market share.
- ❖ . Growth may be proactive change is a necessity for dynamic business environment.
- ❖ Growth refers to in terms of expansion business, increase manpower employment, diversification and acquisition of business and create unknown risky paths in this way organization looks for survival, profitability and growth of the business activities.

Profitability

- ❖ Profitability is the vital goals of a business organization.
- ❖ Profit is the sole motive of the business enterprise.
- ❖ Private business enterprises are operated on behalf of the owners and its benefits also goes to owners of the enterprise.
- ❖ Strategic managers should know how to measure profitability or how to define profitability over the long term or short term of the organization.
- ❖ Profitability clearly indicates of an organization's ability to satisfy the principal; claims and desires of employees and stakeholder of the organization.
- ❖ Strategic mangers are analyses, interpretations of profit of the organization, how it impact on survival of the organization in the future.

Efficiency

- ❖ Efficiency is one of objectives of the business.
- ❖ It helps to business to achieve goals and success of he business
- ❖ Efficiency refers to best utilization of available and scarce resources and brings the highest productivity in business activities.
- ❖ It is useful operation objectives due to effective utilization of economic version of the technical objective which for achieving productivity and designing suitable input and convert into output for effective utilizing of funds, resources, physical facilities and so on in enterprise.

LONG TERM OBJECTIVES OF A BUSINESS

Short run profit maximization is rarely based on the best approach to achieving sustained corporate growth and profitability of the firm. It is recognized by the strategic managers of the firm. Therefore, to achieve long term prosperity purpose strategic managers designed long term objectives. Long term objectives of the firm or company or organization as listed below:

- ❖ Profitability
- ❖ Productivity
- ❖ Competitive position
- ❖ Employees development
- ❖ Employee relationships
- ❖ Public responsibility
- ❖ Technological leadership

Profitability

Profitability is an important functional area of the long-term objectives of the firm. The ability of any business to operate in the long run depends on attaining on acceptable level of profits. Strategically managed firms characteristically have a profit objective usually expressed in return on equity.

Productivity

Productivity is essential need for each strategist in the corporation. Strategic managers try to improve the productivity of their systems. Companies that can improve the input –output relationship normally increase profitability. Productivity objectives are some times stated in terms of desired decreases inmost. This is an equally effective way to increase profitability.

Competitive Position

Competitive position can increases profitability and productivity of the company. Companies or firms or organization's Competitive position reduces the cost of production of the output. The corporate success depends on the firm's competitive position. It is strongly dominated in the market.

Employee Development

It refers to experienced employees are the asset of the organization. For long-term purposes, the company's employees need training for further course of action that effectively and efficiently managed to produce productivity in the competitive position. Therefore, it is one of the major long-term objectives of the organization.

Employee Relationships

All companies actively seek good employee committed relations with organizational environment. Strategic manger should know the employee needs and expectations. Strategic managers take a decision to welfare programme for the employees of the companies. It is only can improved of the employee's relationship in the organization.

Technological Leadership

Technological leadership can gives clear picture of the organization goals and objectives for the long term changes in the business scenario many companies state their objectives in terms of their technological leadership.

Public Responsibility

Business recognizes their social responsibilities towards to customer and society. Public responsibility is buildup long-term images in the society by through providing social work to public.

CHARACTERISTICS OF BUSINESS ENVIRONMENT

Business environment characteristics indicates the challenges, opportunities , threat and weakness of the business.
Major characteristics are listed below:

Environment is Complex

Business environment principally consists of a number of factors , events conditions. These are influenced to different departmental source in the organization. These conditions are not exited in isolation and create entirely new set of influences which are interact with each other. If bring comprehensive influence to business environment. This is difficult to influence to organization. All these factors have to be considered and environment analysis is complex and rigid and totally very difficult to grasp by the functional manager and top level employees in the organization

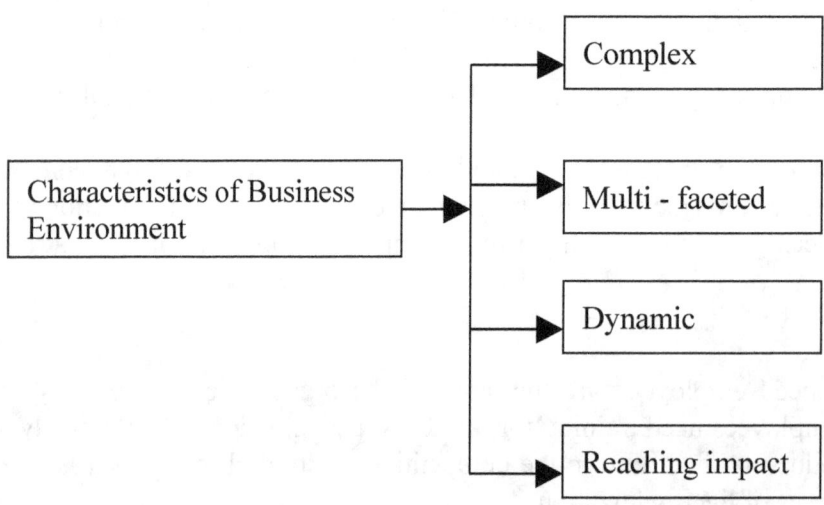

Figure 1.2 indicates the major characteristics business environment

Environment is Dynamic
Business and company environment is constantly changing in different nature. Micro and macro environment factors are influence to business. It impact to change on the business conditions . Dynamic environment is flexible and dynamic nature in company . this is causing due to change. strategic manager can shape strategy and formulate short term and long term objectives.

Environment is Multi – faceted
Observer can shape and observe different character of environment. Observer to observe a particular change or latest development in the business . It is may be viewed different opinion from different observes in the organization. These things are frequently seen when the development happens. All are happy to welcome it and think as it is opportunity for the company even also threat to company.

Environment has a far reaching impact
Environment impact is essential ingredients for strategist to study changes and take appropriate decisions at appropriate time. If strategist neglect to take appropriate decisions at the right time which has a far reaching impact to organization. Survival , growth, and profitability and development to the organization which depends critically in terms of micro and macro factors of the business environment. Environment impact have to be bring new dimensions to business.

ENVIRONMENTAL INFLUENCES ON BUSINESS
The term Environmental analysis is defined as "the process by which strategists monitor the economic, governmental, legal, market, competitive, supplier, technological, geographic, and social cultural settings to determine opportunities and threats to their firms / company / organization".

According to Barry M. Richman and Melvyn Copen
"Environment factors of constraints are largely if not totally external and beyond the control of individual industrial enterprises and their arrangements. These are essentially the 'givers' within which firms and their managements must operate in a specific country and they vary , often greatly from country to country."

According to Glueck and Jauch " The environment includes outside the firm which can lead to opportunities for or threats to the firm. Although, there are many factors , the most important of the sectors are soci – economic , technical , supplier , competitors , and government."

These definitions clearly reveals the following important factors:

❖ strategist looks on the environment changes while to analyze the threats of the business along with searching and offering immense opportunities to business enterprises in the market.

❖ A successful business enterprise has to identify , appraise and respond to the new dimensions of various opportunities and threats in its internal and external environment.

- ❖ Successful business not only recognize business activities even recognize the different elements in the environment.
- ❖ These factors are recognize and adopt their business
- ❖ It continuously monitor and adapt to the new environment
- ❖ Environment analysis helpful to survival and prosper the business activities.

Environment diagnosis principally consists of managerial decisions made by strategist for analyzing the significance of the data like Strengths, weakness, opportunities and threats of the organization to has to design their own strategy for formulation, implementation and controlling the internal environmental factors .

Environmental analysis helps to strategic executive and manager to diagnosis of strategic competitive force and components of strategic management. However, internal environment of the organization is a quite essential and important from the point of view of the environment analysis. It is the cornerstone of the new and exiting business opportunity analysis too.

For instance, the individual life success depends on his innate capabilities like psychological factors, traits and skills. These are to the cope with the environment then will be got success otherwise failure. The survival is the basic elements and success of the business organization, it has depend on its own strengths in terms of resources like money, men, machinery, materials, market and methods as its command. Organization success depends on effective utilization of physical resource, financial resources and human resource skills. These are adaptability to the business environment. Environment is the total of several external and internal forces that affects the functions of business.

Figure – 1.3 : Environment Forces Influences on Business

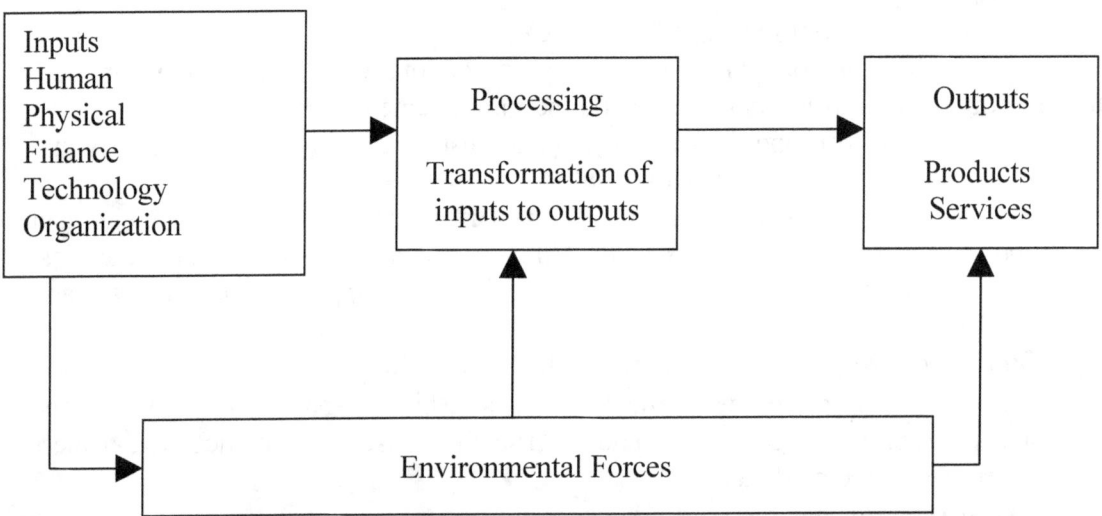

Every business organization principally consists of internal environment factors and set of external environmental factors. Environment factors influence to business directly and indirectly control ,manage and administration of business activities in the organization.

Environment is the basic tool for living all human beings and all living creatures. Human environment consists of family, friends , peers, and neighbors except to natural environment. In additionally includes man – made structures like as buildings , furniture, roads and other physical infrastructure. Individuals do not live in a vacuum.. these are continuously interact with their environment to live and their lives.

Problem in Understanding the Environment Influences

In strategic business environment , strategic managers have face different problems in different circumstance in their business and have to understand the different environmental influence of business as outlined:

❖ The environment problems bring different dimensions to strategic managers. Strategic managers are very difficult to make decisions regarding the different diversity of the business. Strategist will list all conceivable environment influences and very difficult to get overall picture of business environment task. These are emerging problems to strategist and influence to business.

❖ Uncertainty is the second problems encountered by strategic managers. Strategic managers typically claim know the pace of the technological changes and the speed the global network communication. These are more and more faster change now than ever before in business environment. Some of the changes either predictable or unpredictable by the mangers. Mangers can be trying to understand future external influences on business enterprises and this task is very difficult to do so.

❖ Strategic managers are not different from individuals in form of they are coping with complex and rigid. They tend to be simplify complex and rigid problems which are focusing on aspects of the environment. These problems are historically important and confirm prior views of the business. Strategic managers are trying to take risk and simplify the complex and rigid problems in way of find ways and means to breakout bias in the understanding of their environment. It will be still achieving a useful and usable level of analysis in business environment.

Framework to Understand the Environmental Influences

While understanding of the problems in business environment, strategic managers cannot be ignored the real problems of the business. It will be on opportunity to identify a framework for understanding the business environment of the organizations. Environmental factors influence to identify key issues , find the ways for coping with complex and rigid issues and consider as challenging managerial thinking by mangers.

❖ First stage is strategic managers is to know the initial structure and nature of the business organizations in terms of uncertainty. This is relatively either static or shows sign of change. Strategic managers should aware of the simple and complex problems and also know the decision skills for focus the rest of the analysis will be taken in the business environment.

❖ Second stage is the auditing of the environmental influence to business. During this stage, strategic managers aim to identify different environmental influences are likely to affect the organization's development or performance. It is done by assessment of external environmental factors like political , economic , social and technological influences. These are factors bearing at the time of audit of the business. It helpful to strategic managers to develop overall pictures or scenario of possible futures and extent ascertain to changes in the business.

❖ Strategic managers is to moves to focus more towards an explicit considerations of the immediate environment of the organizations, it is the last stage of assessment of the strategic managers. It involves competitive environment and its five forces analysis of competitive environment and identify the key forces at work environment. It is also required to analyze the organization competitive position in form of resources and customers.

ENVIRONMENTAL ANALYSIS

Strategist should aware of the resource capabilities and how to effective utilization of scarce resource capabilities in the company. Environment analysis is to analysis changes pattern and impact of business for decisions. It is considers to opportunity to use and time to anticipated the corporate objectives through proper planning and make optional utilization of available resource in the company. These things helps to strategist to form and develop and give warning early system to prevent threats or to develop strategies which can be turn threat into advantages . It clear indicates future of the company and assessment of the anticipate future

According to Clifton Garvin , environment analysis as "Positive trends in the environment breed complacency. That underscores a basic point : in change there is both opportunity and challenge"

And it is impact on business. Business environment analysis involves the analysis , diagnosis , and take managerial decisions which are likely to better to company. It reduces to length process and time pressure to manages , board of directors in the company. In the case, strategic manager neglect the environment analysis it impact on business changes and ready to face anticipated problems in future . Therefore, the strategic managers can concentrate environmental influence to organization or enterprise.

In general sense, Environmental analysis has three basic goals as outlined .

❖ Environmental analysis must be provided the current and potential changes which are understanding by strategist and bring suitable place in the business environment. Strategist should aware of the existing environment this is must important to company. At the same time , strategist must have take and consider a long tern perspective about the future.

❖ Environment analysis basically provide strategic inputs for strategic decision making, It is not mere collection of data and it is not enough to analysis of the environment. Whatever information collected by the strategist which should be useful to company for making strategic decisions.

❖ Environment analysis is the basic tool and it should make facilitate and foster strategic thinking in the organization. It is typically a rich resource capabilities and ideas which are understanding in the context and purview of the business organization. It should be current challenges , growth, development and opportunities. These wisdoms are bringing by the strategist from the fresh point view of the organization.

ENVIRONMENT INFLUENCE ON SWOT

Environment influence is a part of SWOT analysis. SWOT is acronym of strengths , weakness, opportunity and threats. Threats and opportunities come under the purview of the external environment of the business. Strengths and weakness come under the purview of the internal environment of the business.. These factors are outlined:

- ❖ Opportunity
- ❖ Threats
- ❖ Strengths
- ❖ Weakness

Opportunity

An opportunity is a favourable condition in the business organization's environment which enables it consolidate to resources strengthen its position. Increased company's product and services demand from the customer. It is the best an opportunity to company.

Threat

A threat is an unfavorable condition in the business organization's environment which causes a risk for, or damage to , the organization. Emerging the strong and competitors in the market who are likely to offer stiff competition to the existing companies in the industry, trade and business. This is one of the threats to the organization..

Strength

Strength is an inherent resource capability of the organization or company which can be use and gain to strategic advantages from their competitors in the market. For example strength is the superior research and innovation which help to development of advance skills which can be used for getting new product , new material , new customer in this way achieved to gain competitive strengths in the business.

Weakness

A weakness is an inherent limitations or constraint or problems of the organization. It has to create strategic disadvantages to company or organization. For example a manufacturing company over dependency to single supplier in the market which is potentially risky for company at the time of crisis.

COMPONENTS OF BUSINESS ENVIRONMENT

Exited Business environment of the firms / company or organization can be classified into two broad categories

- ❖ Internal Environment
- ❖ External Environment

Figure – 1.4: Component of Business Environment

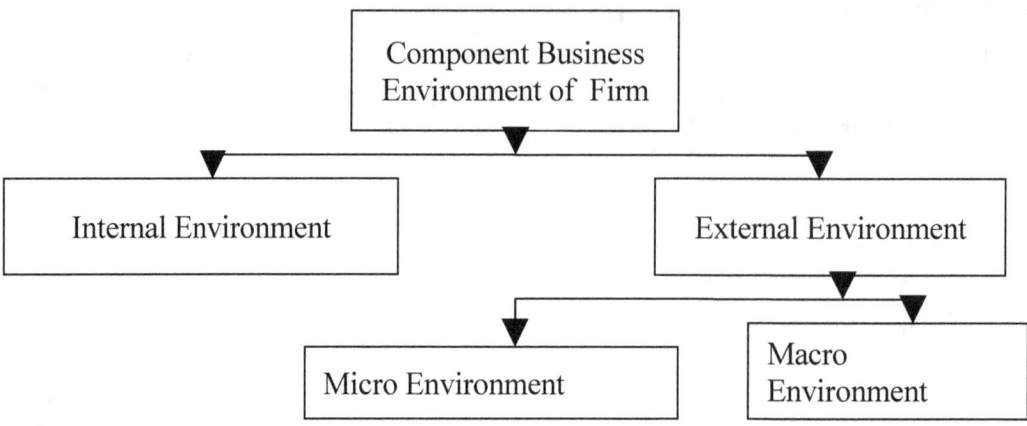

RELATIONSHIP BETWEEN ORGANISATION AND ITS ENVIRONMENT

Relation of business organization and its environment is obvious from the point of analysis of strengths , weakness, opportunity and threats of business. Organisation environment consists of internal environment and external environment. Internal environment factors are easily controllable and manage in the organization. external environment factors are uncontrollable factors due to changes in the legal, social, economic, technical in business enterprise. External environment offers wide range of opportunities , problems, threats and pressures and thereby influence the structure of the business enterprise and its functions. Business enterprise can be treated as subsystem for drawing certain inputs of resource, information and values extracting from the external environmental system. These things transforms into outputs in the form of products and services , goals and satisfactions and exchange of proper ideas and it transmits to business enterprise.

Figure – 1 .5 : Relation Between Organization And Its Environment

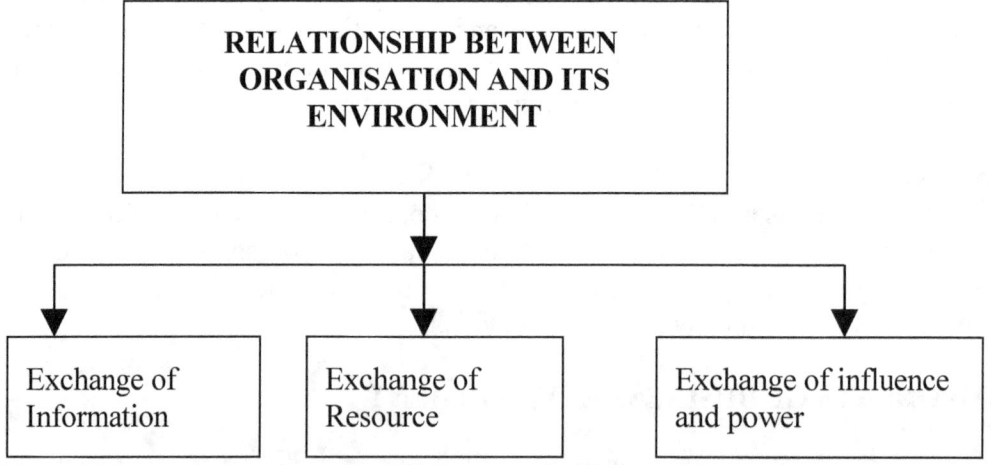

Figure 1.5 indicates the relation between organization and its environment as listed below:

❖ Exchange of Information
❖ Exchange of Resource

❖ Exchange of Influence and Power

Exchange of Information

It refers to data or information is exchanged with business enterprise and its internal and external environment . Exchange of information occurs in the following ways are listed below:

❖ Business organization scans the external environment and internal environment components and their behavior , changes and thereby generates important information and valuable uses for business and make proper planning , decision making and control of environment variables in the organization.

❖ Business organization structure and functions are adjusted with the external environment information.

❖ Generation of external environment information is complex and it is one of the major problem and it involves uncertainty to business organization.

❖ A business project look for current information and future information which are relating to demography, competition, technical , legal , political and government policies and procedures.

Apart from the collecting information, a business organization itself transfer information in the following ways:

❖ Organization transfer its own information to several external agencies either voluntarily , inadvertently or legally.

❖ Other organizations and interest individuals are also approached to business organization to obtain valuable information which relating with functions, products and services and social responsibility towards stakeholders of the company.

❖ An organization collect its own information in form of annual reports , occasional advertisements and media reports etc..

❖ An business organization is legally or otherwise bind to supply valuable information to government, society, financial institution, shareholders, creditors, debtors, investors , employees , trade unions , business bodies and the like.

Exchange of Resource

Exchange resource is the second and dominate relationship with the business enterprise and its environment . exchange of resources involves in the following ways in the business:

❖ Business enterprise receives inputs like finance, materials , manpower, equipment and labor force from the external and internal environment via contractual and other arrangements.

❖ Organization employees is very important due to conversion of these inputs(raw materials) into outputs like products and services

❖ Organization interacts with supplier for purposefully of getting of inputs. For this purpose, an organization does not depend on single supplier and collaborates sometimes with other organization in the process of ensuring a consistent supply of quality inputs.

❖ An organization is also dependent on the external environment factors for disposal of its products and services to wide range of clients and customers.

❖ Disposal of products and services are involved to interaction process external environment for perceiving the needs of the external environment and catering to them , in this way satisfying the expectations and demands of clients ,customers , employees , shareholders , creditors , suppliers, local community, general public and so on.

❖ These above mentioned groups are tended to press on the organization for meeting their expectations, needs and demands and for upholding their value and interests in organization resources.

INTERNAL ANALYSIS OF THE ORGANISATION / COMPANY

Formulation of an effective and efficient strategy has based on a clear definition of organization mission, an accurate assessment of the external environment and through internal analysis of the organization. Organization requires success it needs at least three ingredients. They are as listed:

❖ Strategy must be consistent with conditions in the competitive environment

❖ Strategy must place realistic requirements on the organization / company's internal resources and capabilities.

❖ Strategy must be carefully formulated, implemented, controllable and executed.

Internal analysis of the organization is to difficult and challenging one to strategist. An internal analysis has leads to design a realistic organization profile. It frequently involves tradeoff, value system judgments, educated and skilled guess as well as objective and standardized analysis. A systematic internal analysis leads to main objective of the organization profile. It is essential to develop strategy and design a realistic mission for achievement of the strategy.

Internal analysis of the organization must identify the strategically strengths, opportunities, weakness and threats that are based on organization strategy. Organizational analysis identifies suitable strategy that based on the SWOT analysis.

Internal analysis can be achieved by first identifying key internal factors like value system, mission objectives, management structure and nature, integrated power relationship, human resource, company/organization image and brand equity, physical assets, R&D, technological capabilities, marketing resource and financial resource factors and secondly by evaluating these factors.

THE VALUE OF SYSTEMATIC INTERNAL ASSESSMENT

The value system of internal assessment is essential from the point of view of strategy formulation by the experienced strategist of the organization / company. The value system applies to either large or small business concern. It is critical in developing a successful business strategy. Regardless of the favorable opportunities in the environment, a strategy must be considered the essential internal strengths, weaknesses, opportunities and threats of the organization if such opportunities are to be maximized for accomplishment of goals.

The value systematic internal analysis is particularly essential in small business organizations. Small business organizations are faced lot of problems like limited resource and markets. These organizations are flexible and capable to capture selected markets and effectively channel their limited resource and maximize these limited market opportunities. Internal analysis is the basis objectives of the organization.

Steps/Process in the Development of a Organizational / Company Profile

Company / organization profile   focus on determination of strengths and weakness of the strategic environment of the business. Identifying and evaluating strategic internal factors are based to accomplish to organization future strategy. The major steps are important to development of an organization / company profile. They are listed below:

Stage one   ------------------------   Identification of Strategic Factors

Stage two   ------------------------   Using Value Chain Analysis

Stage three   ------------------------   Evaluations of strategic internal factors

IDENTIFICAION OF STRATEGIC FACTORS

An important identification of strategic factors approach as listed below:
1. Functional approach
2. The value chain approach

FUNTIONAL APPROACH

Functional approach refers to Organization basic capabilities; characteristics, swot analysis and limitation are the key strategic factors. Functional approach key strategic factors are as follows:
- ❖ Marketing
- ❖ Finance and accounting
- ❖ Production /operation/ technical
- ❖ Human resource development
- ❖ Organization of general management

Marketing

Marketing deals with the following issues:
- ❖ Organization's products / service;   product life cycle and marketing strategy.
- ❖ Concentration of sales in few products or   little customer segmentation.
- ❖ Ability to gathered information about the market.
- ❖ To know the market share or sub market share.
- ❖ Product/service mix and expansion potential: to know the life cycle of key products; to know the profit or loss of the product/service.

- ❖ To clearly know the channel of distribution; number, coverage, and control.
- ❖ To maintain effective sales organization: to find out knowledge about the customer needs.
- ❖ To improve product/service quality with image and reputation of brand name.
- ❖ Efficient and effective utilization of available resource for effective sales promotion and advertising.
- ❖ To aware of the pricing strategy and pricing flexibility.
- ❖ To effective monitoring and feedback of the marketing functions and expansion of product
- ❖ Effective implementation of after sales service and follow up.
- ❖ To keep standards, goodwill and brand loyalty.

Finance and Accounting

Finance and accounting functions are as follows:
- ❖ Ability to raise short term and long-term capital: either debt or equity.
- ❖ To maintain good corporate level resource.
- ❖ To know the cost of capital relative to industry and competitors
- ❖ Tax consideration
- ❖ To build up effective relationship with owners, investors, financial institution and stock holders.
- ❖ To know the leverage position: capacity to utilization financial strategies, like lease or sale and lease back.
- ❖ To aware of the cost of entry and barriers of the entry.
- ❖ To know the price earning ration
- ❖ Present working capital position of the organization.
- ❖ Effective cost control and ability to minimize cost of expenditure for production of goods and service.
- ❖ Financial size of the organization.
- ❖ Efficient and effective accounting system for cost, budget, and profit planning of the organization.

Production/Operation/Technical

Production or operation or technical are as follows:
- ❖ To know the present raw material cost and availability
- ❖ Inventory control system of the organization.
- ❖ Location facilities; layout and utilization facilities.
- ❖ Technical efficiency and effective utilization of technical resource in the organization.
- ❖ Effective use and implementation of subcontracting.
- ❖ Degree of vertical integration in terms of value added and profit margin of the product.
- ❖ To know the efficient and cost benefit of production techniques.

- ❖ Effective utilization and implementation of operation control procedure: design, scheduling, purchasing, quality control and efficiency.
- ❖ To know the costs and technological competencies relative to industry and competitors.
- ❖ Research development, innovative, advance ethnological development.
- ❖ Patents, trademarks and similar legal protection for their organization products/service.

Human Resource Development

Human resource development functions are as outlined:
- ❖ Effective management of the human resource in the organization.
- ❖ Improvement of employee skill and morale.
- ❖ Labor relations costs compared to industry and competition from present industry scenario.
- ❖ Efficient and effective formulation and implementation and controlling of the policies.
- ❖ Effective utilization of incentive to motivate employees' performance.
- ❖ To know the ability to level peaks and valleys of employment.
- ❖ To regulate employee turnover and absenteeism.
- ❖ Specialized skills and experience.

Organization of general management

Organization of general management functions are listed below:
- ❖ To know the organization structure.
- ❖ Organization image and prestige to public world.
- ❖ Organization record for achieving goals and objectives.
- ❖ Effective utilization of resource and overall organization control system.
- ❖ To effective monitoring organization cultural climate.
- ❖ Effective utilization of systematic procedure and tools and techniques in decision-making.
- ❖ To know the top management skills, capabilities and interest.
- ❖ Effective implementation strategic planning system.
- ❖ To keep and maintain intra organization synergy (multibusiness)

Some of which would be the focus of internal analysis in most business organization.

Organization is not likely to consider all of the factors are potential strengths or weakness. Strategist has develop or review the factors which are important for successful of the organization.

For the Analysis of the organization, firstly, a strategist has to analyze the past trends like sales, costs and profitability. These trends are the major importance in identification of the internal factors of the organization. Further this identification should be based on a clear picture of the nature of the organization's sales trends. An anatomy of past trends has broken down by product lines channels of distribution of goods and service into different segmentation   of   key customers, geographical region and sales approach should be developed in detail. A similar anatomy of past trends should focus on costs and profitability. Strategist has to conduct detailed investigation of the organization's performance history that helps isolate internal factors influencing to sales, costs and profitability or their interrelationships. The above factors are important in future strategy decisions.

Identification of strategic factors also requires an external focus of the organization.   Strategist isolates key internal factors through analysis of past and present performance like industry conditions / trends and comparisons with competitors. In addition, strategic internal factors are often selected for in depth evaluation because organizations are contemplating expansion of products or markets, diversification.   Strategist carefully   scrutinizes the industry under consideration of current competitors. This is a key means of identifying strategic factors, if an organization is evaluating its capabilities more into unfamiliar markets.

THE VALUE CHAIN APPROACH

Value chain approach developed by Michael Porter, he wrote a book "competitive advantage" which identified the value chain approach of the organization.   A value chain approach is a systematic way of viewing the serious activities of the organization performs to provide a product to its customers. Figure 1.5 highlights the typical value chain approach of the organization. The value chain disaggregate an organization into its strategically relevant activities in order to understand the behavior of the organization's cost and its existing or potential source of differentiation. An organization gains competitive advantage by performing primary and support activities, these activities are more important strategically.

Every organization can be viewed as value chain approach. Value chain approach   as a collection of value activities that are performed to design, produce, market, deliver and support its product. The basic categories of value activities can be grouped into two broad types. They are as listed below:
- ❖ Primary activities
- ❖ Support activities

Primary Activities

Primary activities   are those involved in the physical creation of the product and service in the organization. Its delivery of goods and service and marketing to ultimate buyer and it's providing after sales support to buyer. These activities are supporting to organization that provide inputs or infrastructure to the business.

Figure 1.6: Identifying the Primary Activities of the Value Chain

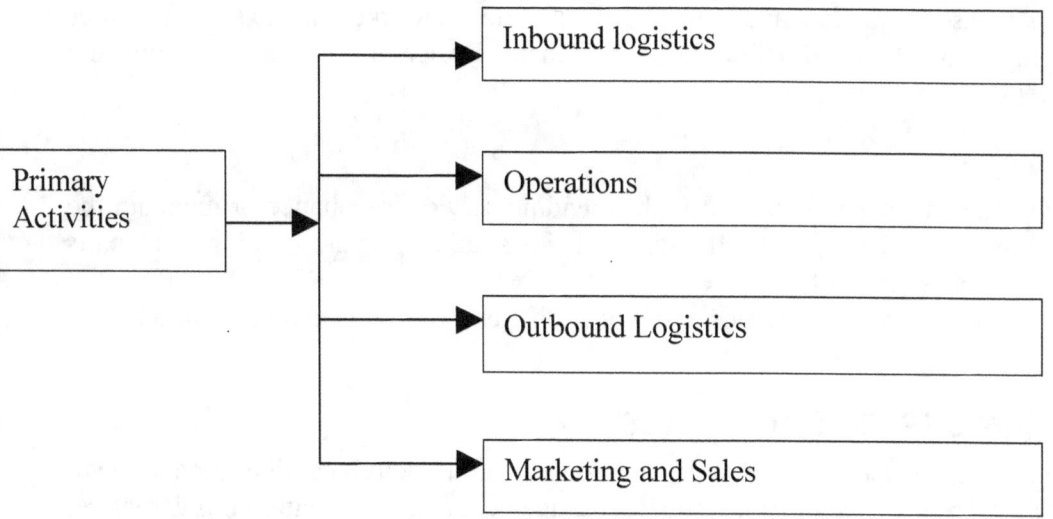

Identifying Primary Activities

Primary activities principally compose of five activities. They are as outlined:

- ❖ Inbound logistics
- ❖ Operations
- ❖ Outbound logistics
- ❖ Marketing and sales
- ❖ Service

Identifying of the primary value activities requires the isolation of activities that are technologically and strategically distinct in the organization. They are five basic categories of the primary activities as listed below:

Inbound Logistics

Inbound logistic activities are associated with receiving, storing and dissemination inputs to the product like material handling, warehousing, inventory control, vehicle scheduling and returns to suppliers.

Operations

Operations activities are associated with transforming inputs into the product form, like machining, packaging, assembly, equipment maintenance, testing printing and facility operations in the organization.

Outbound Logistics

Outbound activities are associated with collecting, storing and physically distributing the product to buyers like finished products warehousing, material handling, delivery vehicle operation, order processing and scheduling.

Marketing and Sales

Marketing and sales activities are associate with providing a means by which buyers can purchase the product and inducting them to do so. Marketing and sales activities are advertising, promotion, sales force, quoting, channel selection, channel relations and pricing strategy of the organization.

Service

Service activities are associated with providing service to enhance or maintain the value of the product. Service activities are like installation, repair, training, and parts supply and product assessment.

The primary activities most deserving of further analysis depend on the particular Industry.

IDENTIFYING SUPPORT ACTIVITIES

Support value activities arise in any one of four activities like procurement, technology development, and human resource management and organization infrastructure. These categories can be identified or disaggregated by isolating technologically or strategically distinct activities. Identifying support activities often overlooked as sources of competitive advantage. Support activities are listed below:

- ❖ Procurement
- ❖ Technology development
- ❖ Human resource management
- ❖ Organization infrastructure

Procurement

Procurement activities are involved in obtaining purchased inputs like raw materials, purchased services and machinery or so on. Procurement stretches across the entire value chain; therefore, it supports every activity-closely relating to purchased inputs of some kind. Different people typically perform with many discrete procurement activities in an organization.

Technology development

Technology development activities are involved in desiring the product like creating and improving quality of the products and service. Technological development is closely relating to innovation of new products and service of the organization. We shall tend to think of technology in terms of the product or manufacturing process. However, every activity of the organization performs and involves a technology. Organization has developed own research and development department for performing to innovation of new product and service.

Figure - 1.7: Support Activities Of The Value Chain

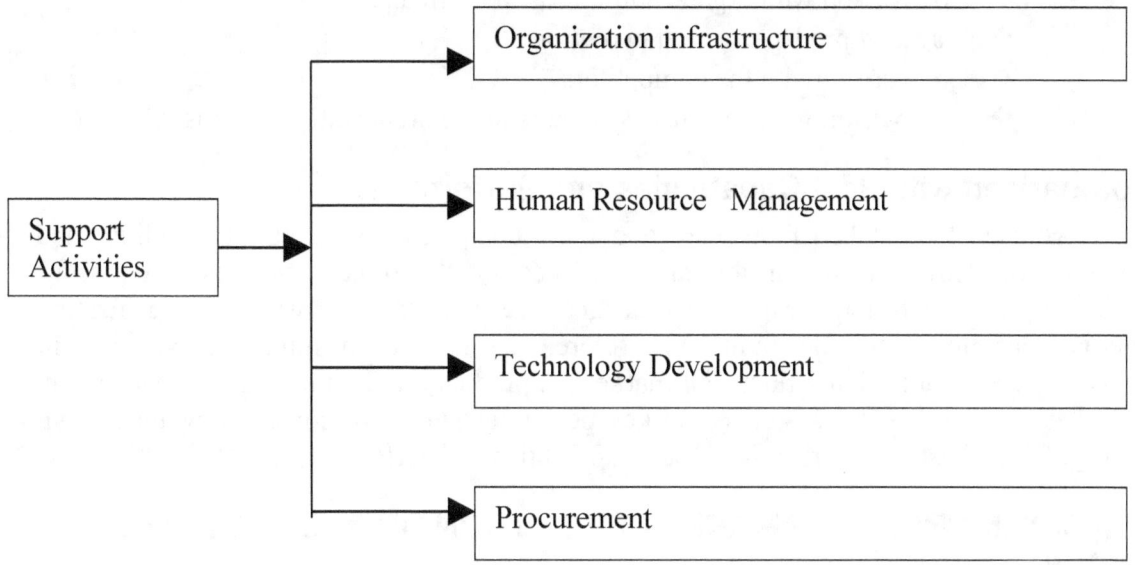

Human Resource Management

Human resource management activities are necessary to ensure the recruitment, training and development of employees in the organization. Every activity involves human resources. Therefore, human resource management activities can control and mange across the entire chain.

Organization Infrastructure

Organization infrastructure activities are such activities as general management, accounting, legal, finance, strategic planning and all others developed organization specific primary activities or support activities but essential to the entire chain's operation.

USING VALUE CHAIN IN INTERNAL ANLYSIS

The value chain provides a useful approach to organization to guide and monitor systematically evaluation of the strengths, weakness, and opportunity and threatens.   An organization provides to distinct value activities like primary and supporting activities. The strategist has identified key internal factors for further examination as potential sources of competitive advantage.

EVALUTION OF STRATEGIC INTERNAL FACTORS

The major objective of internal analysis   is a careful determination of an organization's strengths and weakness. An internal analysis   generates a long list of resources and capabilities have provided little to help in strategy formulation. Instead, internal analysis must identify and evaluate a limited number of strengths and weaknesses

29

relative to the opportunities targeted in the organization's present and future competitive environment.

Strategist evaluates the key internal strengths and weaknesses. He has considered four important basic perspectives. They are as follows:

- ❖ Comparison with organization's past performance
- ❖ Stages of product /market evolution
- ❖ Comparison with the competitors
- ❖ Comparison with key success factors in the organization's industry.

Comparison with Past Capabilities and Performance

Strategist has taken more care about the comparison with past capabilities and performance. However, the historical experience of the organization as a basis for evaluating internal factors. Strategic Managers are most familiar with the organization internal capabilities and constraints. Therefore, they have been immersed over time in managing the organization's financial, marketing, production facilities, sales organization, financial capacity, control systems, and key personnel. Organization has developed own strategy on the basis comparison with past capabilities and performance.

STAGES IN PRODUCT / MARKET EVOLUTION OR PRODUCT LIFE CYCLE

Product life cycle is the second factor to ascertainment of strengths and weakness of organization. Stages in product life cycle are essential from the point of view of successful of the organization. As a result, strategist can use changing patterns associated with different stages in product lifecycle / market evolution as a framework for identifying and evaluating the organization's strengths and weakness.

There are four major stages of product life cycle / market evolution. They are as below:

- ❖ Introduction
- ❖ Growth
- ❖ Maturity
- ❖ Decline/Saturation

And typical changes in functional capabilities often associated with business success at each stage of the development of product /market cycle.

Strengths are needed in the growth stage because of rapid growth brings competitor into the market. This stage involves with brand recognition, product or market differentiation and the financial resources to support both heavy marketing expenses and affect the price competition and effective cash flow can be key strengths at this stage.

As the product/market moves through a "shakeout" phases and into the maturity stage, this stage market growth continues but at a decreasing rate the number of market segments begins to expand, while technological change in product.

While the products markets move toward a saturation decline stage, this stage strengths and weakness center on cost advantages, superior supplier or customer relationships and financial control.

Comparison with competitors

A major focus in determining organization strengths weaknesses is the comparison with potential competitors. Organization in the similar industry often have different marketing potential skills, financial resources, operating facilities and locations, technical know how, brand image, levels of integration, managerial talent. And so on. These different internal capabilities can become relative strengths or weaknesses depending on the strategy of the organization to select. In selection strategy, strategist should compare the organization `s key internal capabilities with those of its rivals, thereby isolating key strengths or weaknesses.

Success factors in the industry

The key determinant success factor in the industry may be used to identify the internal strengths and weaknesses of the organization. By scrutinizing industry competitors, as well as customer needs, vertical industry structures, channels of distribution costs barriers to entry, availability of substitutes, and supplier. A strategist seeks to determine whether organization's current internal capabilities represent strengths or weakness in the new competitive factors.

QUANTITATIVE VERSUS QUALITATIVE APPROACHES IN EVALUATING INTERNAL FACTORS OF THE ORGANISATION

Numerous quantitative tools are available for evaluating selected internal capabilities of a term. Ratio analysis is useful for evaluating selected financial, marketing and operating factors. The organization's balance sheet and income statement are important sources from which to derive meaningful ratios.

Quantitative tools cannot be applied to all internal factors and the normative judgments of key planning participants may be used in evaluation.

EXTERNAL ENVIRONMENT

The concept of external environment is important for every kind of business operation. External environment is an attempt to understand the outside forces of the organizational boundaries that are helping to shape of the organization. External environment clearly considerable bearing on that which transpires will in. The external environment can provide both facilitating and inhibiting influences on organizational performance. Key dimension of the external environment principally consists of a micro environment and a macro environment.

Exhibit 1.8. External Environment

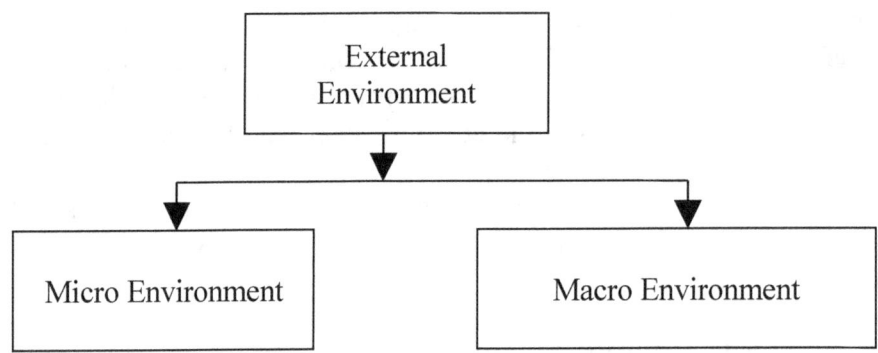

External environment of the business can be categorized into two broad categories as outlined

- Micro Environment
- Macro Environment

Micro environment of business enterprise refers to study on small area or immediate periphery of the business organization. Micro environment directly or regularly influence to business organization. It analyses the following important factors:

- ❖ Human resource (Employees) of the firm, their characteristics and how they are organized in the firm.
- ❖ It analyses the customer base of firm who are major and minor clients of business.
- ❖ It analyses the way of raising of finance of the firm.
- ❖ It analyses who are the suppliers of raw materials and how are the supply chain network between the supplier and firm being developed?
- ❖ It analyses the local communities of firm where its operating.
- ❖ It analyses the direct competition from the competitors and how they perform in business.

Macro environment study the overall issues of firms and broader dimensions. It principally consists of economic , technological , political legal and socio- cultural. Macro environment issues are outlined:

- ❖ It analyses the who are their competitors in the competitive world in which how they are operate and know what are threats from the competitors.
- ❖ It analyses which areas of technology become pose a threat to current product and services and find the reasons for threat.
- ❖ To analyses the bargaining power of suppliers and customers.
- ❖ It analyses nature of competition and how to face the threat and weakness of the firm.

Environmental Scanning
Environmental scanning is also known as Environmental Monitoring. It is the process of gathering information regarding firm's/ organization's or company, analyzing it and

forecasting the impact of all predictable trends in environmental changes. Successful marketing always depends on its environmental scanning and its marketing programmes which depends on its environmental changes.

MICRO / OPERATING ENVIRONMENT

The micro / operating environment consist in the organization or company's immediate environment that affects the performance of the organization / company. These included as listed below:

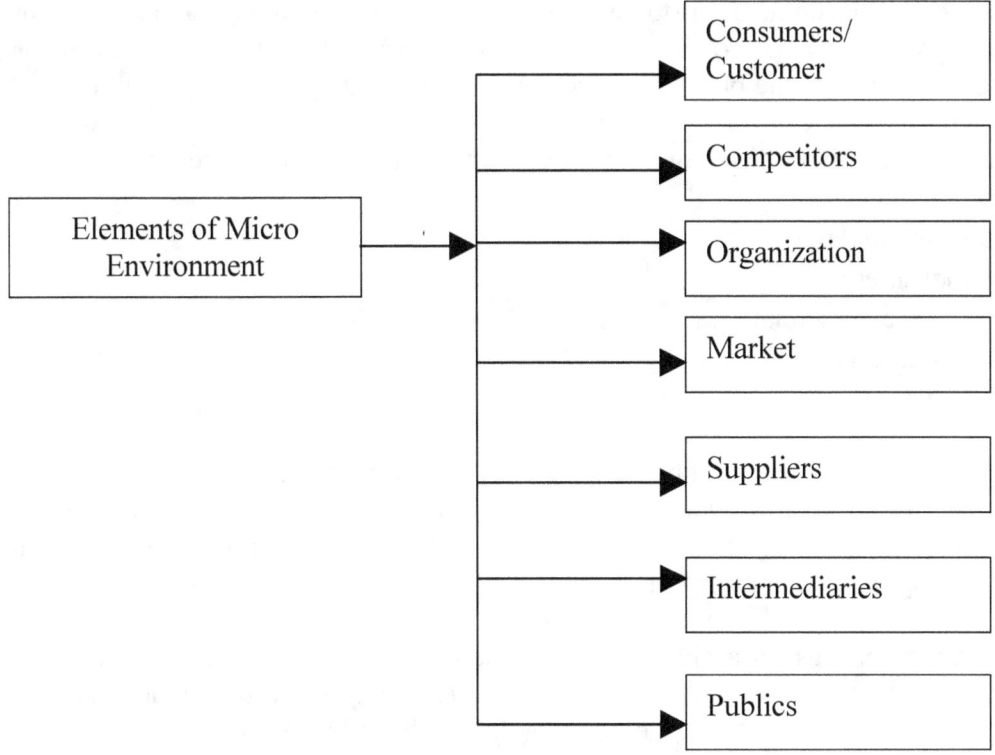

It is quite important that micro/operating environment factors are more intimately linked with organization or company than macro / remote environment factors. The micro/operating forces need not necessarily affect all organizations in a particular industry. Some of the micro factors particular to be affected organization. For instance, an organization that depends on a supplier may have a supplier environment that is quite entirely different from that of an organization whose supply source is also different. When competing organizations in an industry have the same microelements, the relative success of the organization depends on their relative effectiveness in dealing with these elements.

Suppliers

Supplier is the important force of the micro/operating environment of an organization or company i.e., the supplier those who supply the inputs like raw materials and components to the organization. The major and important of reliable source / sources of supply to the smooth function of a business is very important. Uncertainties are generated the several supply problems like maintenance of inventory, delay of supply of inventory to organization.

Many organizations give high importance to vendor development, vertical integration for solve the supply problem. Organization has depended on a single supplier is a risk factor due to   a strike, lockout or any other production problem of the supplier. Always an organization has depended on several supplier of the same raw material.   Similarly, a change in attitude   or behavior of the suppler may also affect the organization.   Hence, multiple sources of supply often help reduce such risks. The supply management assumes more importance in a scarcity environment.

Customers

The major task of business is to create and development of customers. A business can exist only because of its customers. Customers are the people who pay money to acquire or buy an organization products in the form of goods   and services.   Monitoring the customer's behavior is a prerequisite for the business success. Consumer is the one who will ultimate use of company's products and services.

Organization may have different kinds of customers. They are listed below:

❖ Individual
❖ Households
❖ Industries
❖ Other commercial establishments
❖ Governments
❖ Other institutions

According to Peter Drucker the aim of business is to create and retain customer.

For instance, the customers of an auto-mobile sphere parts manufacturing organization may include individual automobile, owners, automobile manufactures, public, private sector transport undertakings and other transport operators.

Organization depends on a single customers is often much difficulty and risky task. Organization cannot survival without survival. Therefore, it may place the organization in a poor bargaining position, apart from the risks of losing business result to winding up of business by the customer or due to the customers switching over to the competitors of the organization.

The strategic choice of the customer segments should be made by considering a number of factors including the relative profitability, dependability, and stability of demand, growth prospects and the extent of competition.

Firms should know about who are their customers, expectations and buying patterns.

Competitors

An organizations competitor includes not only the other organization which market the same or similar products but also those who compete for the discretionary income of the customers. For instance, the competition for a organization's televisions may not come from other televisions manufactures but also from two –wheeler, refrigerators, cooking ranges, stereo sets and so on and from organizations offering saving and investment scheme like banks, unit trust of India, companies accepting deposits or issuing shares or debenture etc.   This competition among those products maybe described as desire competition as the primary task here is to influence to the basic decision of the consumer.   Such desires competition is generally very high in countries characterized by limited disposable incomes and many unsatisfied desires because of wants are unlimited.

If the consumer decides to spread his discretionary income and recreation he will still be confronted with a number of alternatives to select from such computer., stereo, two in one, three in one. The competition among such alternatives that satisfy a particular category of desire is called generic competition.

An implication of these demands is that a marketer should strive to create primary and selective demand for his products.

Marketing Intermediaries

The immediate environment of a organization may principally consist of a number of marketing intermediaries which are "organizations that aid the organization in promoting, selling and distributing its goods to final buyers". In many cases, the customers are not aware of the manufacturer of the products and services they want buy. They want to buy products and services from the local intermediaries.

The marketing intermediaries are as outlined:
- ❖ Middlemen
- ❖ Agents
- ❖ Merchants
- ❖ Marketing agenesis
- ❖ Advertising agencies
- ❖ Marketing research firms
- ❖ Media
- ❖ Consulting firms

Publics

Public is the one important marketing intermediaries for promoting, advertising, channeling, selling the organization's product into different segmentation. If public accept the product of the organization, definitely it will successful in the market, suppose product is rejected by the public definitely it will close the company.

Organization

- ❖ Organization involves the group of employees who are working different positions and different nature of jobs. These employees come from the outside. Individual employee interest is different and varied
- ❖ An organization has consist of several non specific factors in the organization's environment which are affecting its activities. Owners, Board of Directors and employees are likely to influence to organization.
- ❖ Owners are individuals, shareholders, groups, or organizations who have a major stake in the organization. Owners are vested interest in the well being of the company.
- ❖ Board of directors are originate in companies formed under the companies Act,1956. The board of directors is elected by the shareholders. Board of directors are the responsible and in charge of the organization also overseeing the general

management of the organization. In this way , Board of directors have to ensure that run business in best serves to the shareholders' interest.

❖ Employees are the asset of the organization who   are intend to work in an organization. Employees are the major force of the organization. Work culture, values and goals of the organization are important to employees. Therefore, they differs in terms of beliefs , education, attitudes, and capabilities. When there is difference with employee goals and manager's goals that time entire organization will be suffered due to different attitude and reactions about in organization.

Market

Market is to essential   and important to organization. The market structure is to be studied in the form of its actual and potential size, its growth and also attractiveness of product and services of the organization. Strategist should be studied the trends and development and key success factors of the market. The major marketing issues are outlined :

❖ What is the cost structure of the market?
❖ What is the price sensitivity of the market?
❖ What is the existing distribution system of the market?
❖ Is the market growing/ mature/ decline?

MACRO / REMOTE ENVIRONMENT

Macro environment is largely external to the business enterprise. Macro environment factors are uncontrollable factors and beyond the direct influence and control of the organization. Its factors are powerfully influence to its functions. External environment consists of individuals, groups, agencies, organizations, events , conditions and forces . These are frequently contacted by the organization for its functions.   It establishes good interaction and interdependent relations in form of conducts business transitions . designs, and administrative and provide to appropriate strategies and policies are cope with and make to changes. Other wise negotiates and buildup its future by using of the macro environment factors.

The macro/remote environment principally consists:

❖ Economic environment
❖ Political environment
❖ Legal environment
❖ Socio-cultural environment
❖ Demographic environment
❖ Natural environment
❖ Physical and technological environment
❖ Technological Environment
❖ Global or International environment

Macro environment force is uncontrollable i.e. uncontrollable factors of business organizations.

Exhibit – 1. 9 : Macro Environment Elements

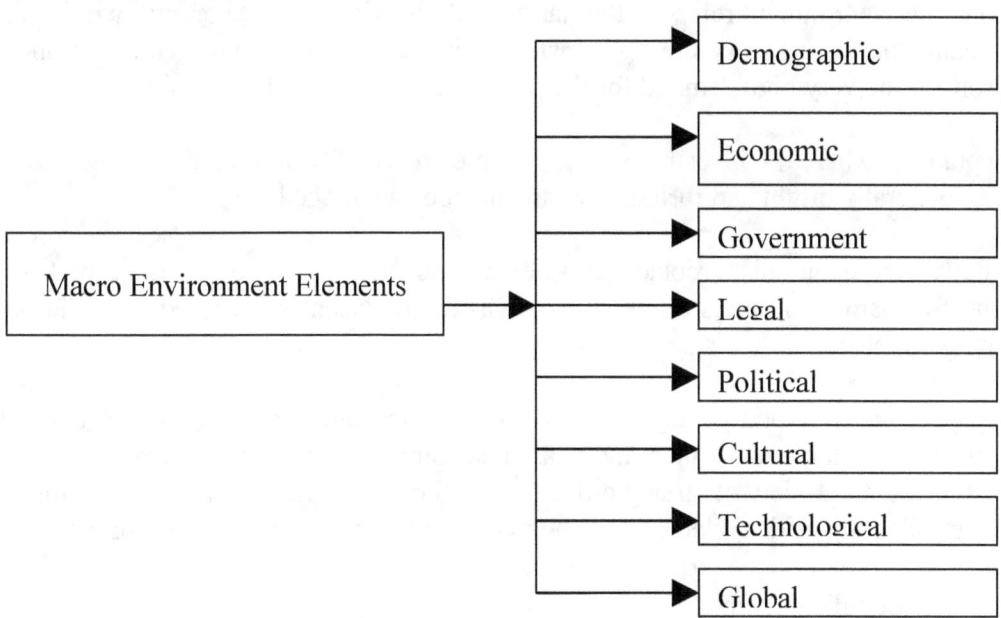

ECONOMIC ENVIRONMENT

The economic environment constitutes to economic conditions, economic polices, and the economic system that is the important external factors of business.

The economic conditions of the country include:

- ❖ Nature of the economy of the country
- ❖ The general economic situation in the region , conditions in resource markets like money, material , market raw material components , services , supply markets and so on which influence the supply of inputs to the organization, their costs, quality, availability and reliability of supply of products and services.
- ❖ It determines the economic strength and weakness in the market.
- ❖ Purchasing of power of the individual depends upon the economic factors like current income, price, savings , circulation of money, debt and credit availability.
- ❖ People income distribution pattern analyses the market possibilities and impacts on enterprise.
- ❖ Development process of the country
- ❖ Availability of economic resources of the country
- ❖ The level of the economic income of the country
- ❖ The distribution of income and assets of the country
- ❖ Public finance of the country

These are the very important determinants of business strategy in the organization for formulating, implement and controlling of economic policies.

Economic environment refers to the nature and direction of the economy within which business organization are to operate. For instance, in developing country, the low income maybe reason for the very high demand for the product and services of the business.

In countries where the investments and income are steadily and rapidly rising, business prospects are generally bright and further investments are encouraged.

In developed economics, replacement demand accounts for a considerable part of the total demand for many consumers durables where as the replacement demand is negligible in the developing countries.

Money is the lifeblood of any business organization and the economic system. The economy consists of microeconomics and macroeconomics. Micro and macro elements are important from the point view of strategic decisions. Strategist must scan , monitor, forecast, and assess the following critical elements of the macro and micro economic environment :

- ❖ Economic system
- ❖ Nature of the country economy
- ❖ The monetary and fiscal policies
- ❖ Autonomy of the economy
- ❖ Functions of economics
- ❖ Factors of productions
- ❖ Economic trends and structures
- ❖ Economic policy statements and structure
- ❖ Economic legislation
- ❖ Economic problems
- ❖ Import and export policy
- ❖ Tax rates
- ❖ Interest rates
- ❖ Government budget deficit
- ❖ Consumption pattern
- ❖ Price fluctuations
- ❖ Global movement of labour and capital
- ❖ Stock market trends
- ❖ Coalitions of countries and regional states
- ❖ Availability of credits
- ❖ Inflation trends in country
- ❖ Unemployment trends
- ❖ Foreign country economic conditions
- ❖ Company of Petroleum Exporting Countries (OPEC)) policies.

Economic environment encourages liberalization, privatization and globalization of the economic policies in the business environment. Every country's development is based on the economic environment activities that withheld to the development process of the country.

POLITICAL - LEGAL ENVIRONMENT

Political environment refers political and government and legal environment. It has close relationship with the economic system and economic policy. For instance; the communist countries had a centrally planned economic system. Communist government countries laws are control investment and related matters. There are number of law that regulates the conduct of the business. These laws cover such matter as standards of business and its production and service.

❖ The democracy governments countries law's / act are passed in the parliament. Then they are regulating rules and regulation of business according to the act.

❖ Political stability , responsibility, political ideology and level of political morality, the law and order situation , and practice of the ruling party and major purposefulness and efficiency of the government agencies.

❖ Political agencies nature, its influence to economic and industrial act ivies in the country.

❖ Government policies like fiscal , monetary, industrial , labour , and export and import policies which are influence to specific legal enactments and framework in which the business organization has to function and degree of the effectiveness with these are influenced to formulate and implement policy in the legislature.

The political environment based on the uncertainty. Therefore, demographic countries consist of number political parties. Political parties aren't got clear majority to form a government. In this situation, industry and commerce collapsed their business activities due to hung government. The political parties are unable to formulate stable government, it affect and fluctuate the government Policies. Therefore, business organization and public needed to the stable government.

Elements of Political and legal Environment
There are three important elements are associated with the political and legal environment as listed below:

❖ Government
❖ Legal
❖ Political

Government
❖ Government policies , rules and regulation are controlling and monitoring the business enterprises and its activities in the state.

❖ Secondly, the type of government administration of the state and what is the business policy of state? These things should be evaluated by the strategist from point of view of business.

❖ Strategist should study about the changes in the regulatory framework of the government and impact on the business.

❖ Government tax policies are critical and affect to the business organization in the state.

Legal

- ❖ Sound legal system is the basic requirement for running of the business operating with in the state.
- ❖ Strategist should aware of various business laws which are protecting consumers, competitors, and organization.
- ❖ Business organization should aware of the laws which relevant to companies , competitors, intellectual property, foreign exchange , labor and so on.

Political

- ❖ Political system is also influenced to business and its activities
- ❖ Political pressure groups influence to government and in this way some extent to control and regulate business activities with in the country.
- ❖ Recently , special interest groups and political action committee put pressure to business organization and to pay more attention towards consumer's rights, minority rights, and women rights.
- ❖ Apart from the sporadic movements against certain products and services and some business organization in the state.

SOCIO –CULTURAL ENVIRONMENT

Socio cultural environment is an important factor that should be analyzed while formulating company business strategies. If company's is ignoring the customs, traditions, tastes and preferences and education are all factors that affect business. It consist of factors which are related to human relationships and the impact of social attitudes and cultural values. These are bearing on the business of the organization.

Business organization is a successful due to appropriate strategies effective utilization of socio-cultural environmental factors. Social cultural environment is an important for MNC. Therefore, MNC should study of the social cultural activities of the region, where there are introducing their own business. Even when the people so different cultures use the same basic product, the mode consumption, conditions of use or perceptions of the product attributes may very so much so that the product attributes method of presentation, promoting product may have to varied to suit the characteristic of different market segmentation. Socio-cultural factors are beliefs, values, norms and traditions of the society determine how individuals and organizations should be interrelated.

The difference in language sometimes poses a serious problem, even necessitating a change in the brand name. The value and beliefs associated with colour vary significantly between different cultures. For instance, white indication death and mourning in china and Korea; but some country it expresses happiness and is the colour of the wedding dress of the bride.

Some of the socio cultural factories are influence to operating environment of organization as outlined:

- Social issues like the role of the business in the society, environment pollution, corruption, use of mass media and consumption of products and services which are offered by the company.
- Social attitudes and values issues like social customs , beliefs , rituals and practices, changing life style patterns and materialism are expectations of society from the business.
- Family structure, values and attitudes towards the family and these changes also influence to business and its operation..
- Role of the women, position , nature of responsibilities in society is also influence to business and its operation in market.
- Educational levels, awareness and consciousness of rights and work ethics of the society can be influenced to business and its operation.

Social practice, beliefs and associated factors come in the way of the promotion of the action of certain products, services or ideas, the success of marketing depends to a vary large extent ,on the success in changing social attitudes or value systems.

DEMOGRAPHIC ENVIRONMENT

Demography refers to study of the population. Demographic factors are as below:
- The population size
- Growth rate of population
- Age composition of the population
- Family size
- Economic stratification of the population
- Education levels
- Language
- Caste
- Religion
- Race
- Age
- Income
- Educational attainment
- Asset ownership
- Home ownership
- Employment status and location

These factors are the relevant to the business for formulating and implementing of strategy for controlling and accomplishment of the objectives of the organization.

Demographic factors like size of the population, population growth, rate, age, composition, life expectancy, family size, spatial dispersal, occupational status, employment pattern etc., affect the demand for goods and service.

The growth of population and income result increases demand for goods and services. A rapidly increasing population indicates that a growing demand for many products. For instance, developing countries like India, Pakistan, etc; high population growth rate indicates an enormous increase in labor supply.

The occupational and spatial nobilities of population have implications for business. Labor is easily mobility between different occupations and regions. Its supply will be relatively smooth and this will be relatively and this will affect the wage rate.

If a labor is highly heterogeneous in respect of language, caste and religion, ethnicity, etc., personal management is likely to become a more complex task. The heterogeneous population with its varied tastes, preferences, beliefs, temperaments, etc, gives rise to different demand patterns and calls for different marketing strategies.

Business organization needs to study different demographic issues which are particularly address the following :
- ❖ What democratic trends which will affect the market size of the different types of industry?
- ❖ What democratic trends will represent opportunities or threats?

Interested Domestic Environment Factors To Business
We shall briefly discuss a few demographic factors which are interest of business :
- ❖ Population Size
- ❖ Geographic Distribution
- ❖ Ethnic Mix
- ❖ Income Distribution

Population Size
Size of population is important either small or large to business organization. Companies use population size for critical assessment for customer behavior and changes of the customer behavior and its impact on business. Important issues are outlined which are relating with population:

- ❖ It study the changes in a nation's birth rate and family size.
- ❖ It study the increase and decrease in the total population.
- ❖ It also study he changes effects in terms of rapid population growth on natural resources or food supplies.
- ❖ It also study the life expectancy of infants , youth and old age people.

These issues are very important to company for analysis of demand and supply of products and services. Healthcare companies role is needful for assessment of the product requirement for infants, youth, middle age and old age people.

Geographic Distribution

It refers to geographic region and population shifts from one region of a nation to another or from village/rural areas to urban areas. This is may be an impact on a company's strategic competitiveness in market. Geographic Distribution issues are outlined:

- ❖ Location advantage and government support is also very important to company.
- ❖ In the case, Population is shifted from one region to another region. This is the significant impact on company's qualified workforce and company consider relocation of its skilled human resources.
- ❖ Today, working at home concept and electronically on the information highway have also begun in India in an very small level.

Ethnic Mix

Ethnic mix is also important to company and know eager know changes in ethnic mix in population . assessment and implications of ethnic mix is useful for company and its works force. Ethnic issues are outlined:

- ❖ Company should know the changes in the ethnic mix and its impact to company's product and services.
- ❖ Company should know the new products demand or existing products and services from the different ethnic groups.
- ❖ Company ready to face challenges , treats from ethnic and try to make solutions for these ethnic challenges and treats.

Income Distribution

Income distribution is also one of the important factors of demographic environment. Company is planning to measure changes in incoming distribution, savings patterns for different level of individual. This purpose, company can forecast and assess the changes in income patterns and ready to identify new opportunities for companies.

NATURAL ENVIRONMENT

Natural environment is the study of an important component of the nature i.e., natural environment. Natural environment includes geographical and ecological factors areas below:

- ❖ Natural resource endowments,
- ❖ Weather
- ❖ Climate conditions
- ❖ Topographical factors
- ❖ Location aspects in the global context
- ❖ Port facilities are relevant to business.

Difference in geographical conditions between markets may sometimes call for changes in the marketing mix. Geographical and ecological factors also influence industries which help material index tend to be located near the raw material sources. Climate and weather conditions affect the location of certain industries like the often textile industry.

Ecological factors have recently assumed great importance. The depletion of natural resources, environmental pollution and the disturbance of the ecological balance has caused great concern. Government policies aimed at presentation of environment al purity and ecological balance, conservation of non replenisable resources etc., have resulted in additional responsibilities and problems for business, and some of these have the affect of increasing the cost of production and marketing, externalities have become an important problem of the business has to confront with.

TECHNOLOGICAL ENVIRONMENT

Technological factors some times pose serious problems. A firm that unable to cope with technological changes may not be survived. Further, the differing technological environment of different markets or countries may be called for product modifications.

Technology is the most important elements of the macro environment. Technology is the human being innovation and he has literally wonder. Technology help to human being go to moon, traveling the spaceships, other side of the globe with few hours.

Advances in the technologies have facilitated product improvements and introduction of new products and have considerably improved the marketability of the products.

The fast changes in technologies also create problems for enterprises as they render plants and product obsolete. Today adopt changes in technology to achieve successful in business and industry.

Internet and telecom system is the part of technological development in the world. These things today changed whole world. It changes people and business operation. It leads to many new business opportunities apart from the many existing systems. Technological environment characteristics are outlined:

- ❖ The find of technological change
- ❖ Opportunities are arising out of technological developments.
- ❖ Risk and Uncertain is the major feature of the technological developments.
- ❖ Research and development role to country

Technology and business activities are to be highly considerable, interrelated and interdependent . Technology output/ fruit's available to society through business activities in this way improve the quality of life in the society. Therefore, technology nurtured by business.

Technologies issues relating with companies are listed below:

- ❖ Access to the internet communication facilities which is enable to connect large numbers of employees to work from one place/ home to another place in the globe. Information Highway provide opportunity to strategist to access to richer source of information..
- ❖ It helps to business to business for sales and exchange of goods and services.
- ❖ It provide opportunity to customers with accessing to online shopping through the internet technology.

Key Issues Of Technology
- ❖ Strategist should know what of type technology used by company?

- ❖ Strategist should know the which type of technologies are used in the companies business, products and its services?
- ❖ To know the critical issues in technology and know the operating skills in technology related products and services.
- ❖ To know the availability of technology to organization. And its procedure to get external technology to company for its operations.
- ❖ To know the cost of technology, alternative technology, competitors, design structure T of the technology and production implementation services of the company.
- ❖ To know the companies business applications which are relating to technology.
- ❖ To know the additional technologies which required to companies business. And how to get these additional technologies in the world market.
- ❖ Technology is help to business for formulation of strategy, implementation of strategy and control of the company performance.

Exhibit -1. 10 : Technological Environment of the Company

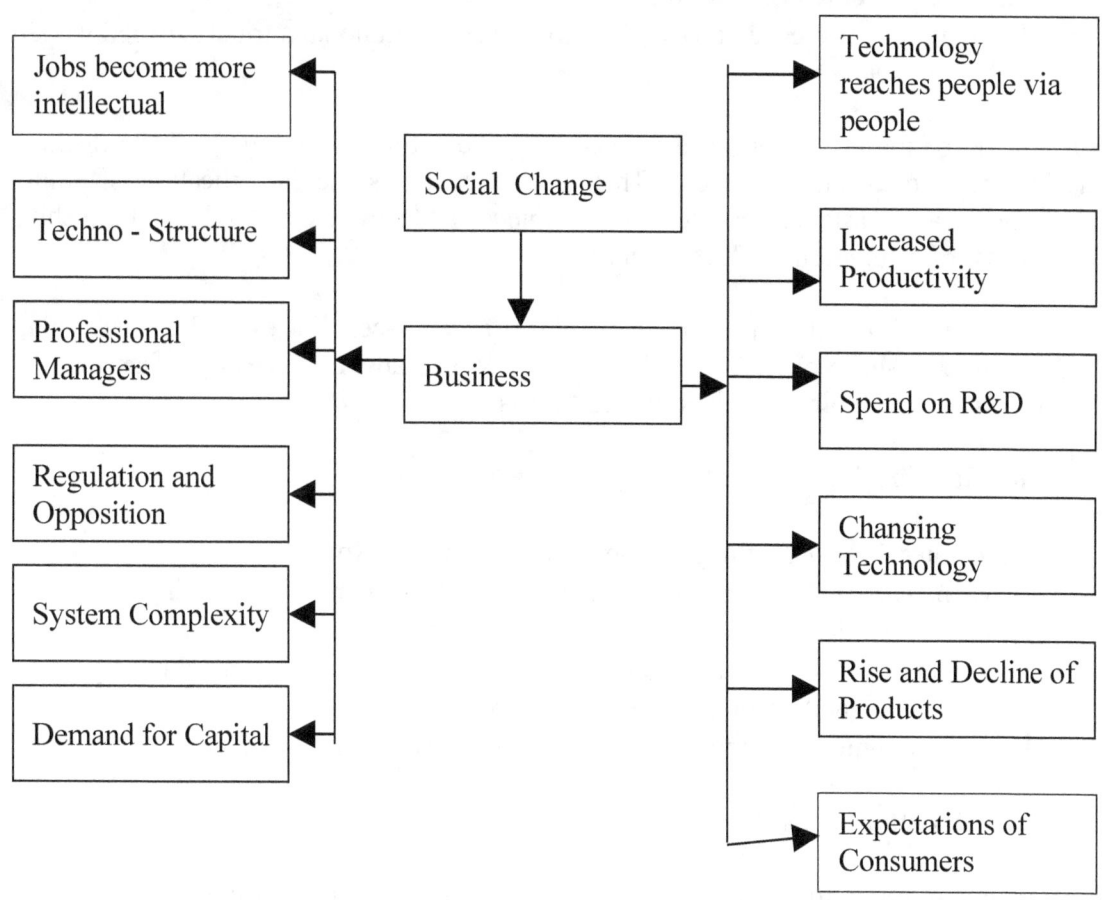

GLOBAL ENVIRONMENT

Global environment is one of the important elements to macro environment of the business. Today competitive scenario changes rapidly and its impact on business of company. For this, reasons, strategist should understand the global environment, its characteristics, functions and merit and demerit to company. Global environment treated as whole world just as village and has changed how individuals and organizations relate to each other. Nowadays, increased offshore operations and changes business operation. these are influence to organization to get project from global clients.

Assessment Of The Global Environment Factors

Assessment of the global environment factors are outlined:

- ❖ To know the potential positive and negative impact of significant international events like a sport meet or a terrorist attack
- ❖ To identify both emerging global markets and global market which are ensuring changing. It includes newly industrialized countries like in Asia. In developing countries that imply the opening of new markets for new products, that's result is to be increased competition from emerging globally competitive companies in India and South Korea and China.
- ❖ To know the difference between in cultural and institutional attributes of individual global markets.

Globalization of markets refers to the process of integrating and merging of the distinct world markets into a single market. This process involves the identification of some common norm, value, taste, preference and convenience and slowly enables the cultural shift towards the use of a common product or service.

A number of consumer products have global acceptance. For example, coca –cola, Pepsi, McDonald's Music of Madonna, MTV, Sony Walkmans, Levis jeans, Indian masala dose, Indian Hyderabadi biryani, Citicorp credit cards etc.

Nature of Globalization

- ❖ It indicates the several things for several people in the world.
- ❖ It is new concept that based on the set of fresh beliefs, working methods, economic, political and socio- cultural relatives in business.
- ❖ It integration with the world economy and open for new and potential huge market for developing and developed countries in the global.
- ❖ It intend to remove all trade barriers among countries in the world.

Characteristics Of a Global Company

Global company refers to operating in more than one country in the world and gains its R&D, production, marketing and financial advantages in terms of costs and reputations that are not available to domestic competitors. Global company is one that has the world market. Minimizes the importance of national boundaries , sources, raises capital and market in this way it will be done the best job.

Global company major characteristics are outlined:

* Global company is a firm which having multiple units that are located in different parts of the world but all linked by common ownership umbrella.
* Global multiple units draw on a common pool of resources like money, credit information , patents , trade names and control systems.
* Global company can be follow common strategy for sell its products in most countries and manufactures in many. Another important fact is that its shareholders and human resources are also based on different nations.

Reasons for Globalization

* Large-scale industrialization enabled mass production. Consequently, the companies found that the size of the domestic market is very small to suffice the production output and thus opted for foreign markets.
* Companies in order to reduce the risk diversity of portfolio of countries.
* Companies globalize markets in order to increase their profits and achieve goals.
* The adverse business environment in the home country pushed the companies to globalize their markets.
* To cater to the demand for their products in the foreign markets.
* The failure of the domestic companies in catering   the needs of their customers pulled the foreign countries to market their products.

International environment is the very important from the point of view of certain categories of business. It is particularly important industries directly depending on imports or exports and import competing industries.

Advantages of Globalization

* Free flow of capital and increase in the total capital employed
* Free flow of technology from developed countries to developing countries
* Increase in industrialization
* Spread production facilities throughout the global
* Balanced development   of world economies
* Increased in production and consumption of outputs
* Commodities available at lower price with high quality
* Cultural exchange and demand for a variety of products in foreign market
* Increased in jobs opportunities and income
* Balanced in welfare and prosperity of the country's economic

Disadvantages of Globalization

- ❖ Globalization kills domestic small business firms
- ❖ Exploits human resources in global firms
- ❖ Leads to unemployed and underemployment in developing countries
- ❖ the customer demand decline in domestic products
- ❖ Decline the income because of unemployment
- ❖ Widening gap between rich and poor
- ❖ National sovereignty at stake
- ❖ Leads to commercial and potential colonialism to poor countries

Why do companies go global?

There are Important reasons for Companies go to global as outlined:

To Gain Access to New Customers

This is the first reason to companies expand into foreign market. It offers potential for increased revenues, profits and long-term growth and becomes an especially attractive option when a company's home markets is mature. Mature industries plan to enter new market, therefore, to access to new customer for their products and service.

To Achieve Lower Cost Enhance the Firms Competitiveness

This is the second reason to domestic companies opt to expanding their market in outside countries. Many companies are driven to sell their products and service in more than country because the sales volume achieved in their own domestic markets is not large enough to fully capture manufacturing economies of scale and experience curve effects and thereby substantially improve a firm's cost competitiveness.

To Capitalize on it's Core Competencies

This is the third factor to companies expand their domestic market into international market. A company with competitively valuable competencies and capabilities may be able to leverage them into a position of competitive advantage in foreign market as well as just domestic markets.

To spread its Business Risk across a Wider Market base

This is the last reason opt companies to expand their domestic market into international market. A company spreads its business risk by operating in a number of different foreign countries rather than depending entirely on operations in its own domestic market.

Except in a few cases, companies in natural resource – based industries such as oil and gas, minerals, rubber and lumber often to find it necessary to operate in the international arena because of attractive raw material suppliers are located in foreign countries.

Speed And Faster Communication Network
Globe thanks to faster communication, speedier transportation, growing financial flows and rapid technological changes due to advanced communication network development.

Reduce transportation costs
Companies often set up overseas plants and machinery to reduce transportation costs. The following development are also responsible for transportation operation of companies:

❖ It happens when increasing emphasis on market forces and growing role for the private sector in all developing countries.

❖ Globalization of firms and industries

❖ The rise of the services sector. It constitute the one of the largest single sector in the world economy.

❖ Rapidly changing technologies which are transforming in the originate nature , organization , an location of international production.

MANIFESTATION OF GLOBALIZATION

Important manifestation of globalization are outlined :

Configuring Any Where In The World
An Global organization can be located in different place in the world and its different types of operations in different countries for supply of raw material, look for consumer markets and low cost lour and manufacturing of products and services in the world .

Interlinked And Independent Economies
Globalization refers to economic welfare of the state and its people for uniquely economically interdependent international environment. Each country's prosperity is dependent on the interlinked with the rest of the world. No nation can not be survival any longer time without existence of the international market and domestic market.

Lowering Of Trade And Tariff Barriers
Global environment brings lowering of trade and tariff barriers to global enterprises in the world. It proposes a new global cooperative arrangements and redefined the role of the state and its industry status. It help towards privatization of manufacturing, services sectors, and less government interference in business decisions and help to private sector to buildup the value added sector in this way to gain market place and competitiveness in the global market. When the lowering of trade and tariff barriers in state which results in available products and services at lower cost with abundant supply of goods and services to ultimate customers.

Infrastructural Resources And Inputs At International Prices
When global firms are entering into global market , it ensure that infrastructural inputs must be available at competitive prices due to availability of cheap labor and other valuable

resources like physical facilities, raw material etc , a global firms take high level risk particularly continuous inflation and high infrastructural costs in the country.

Figure– 1.11 : Manifestation Of Globalization

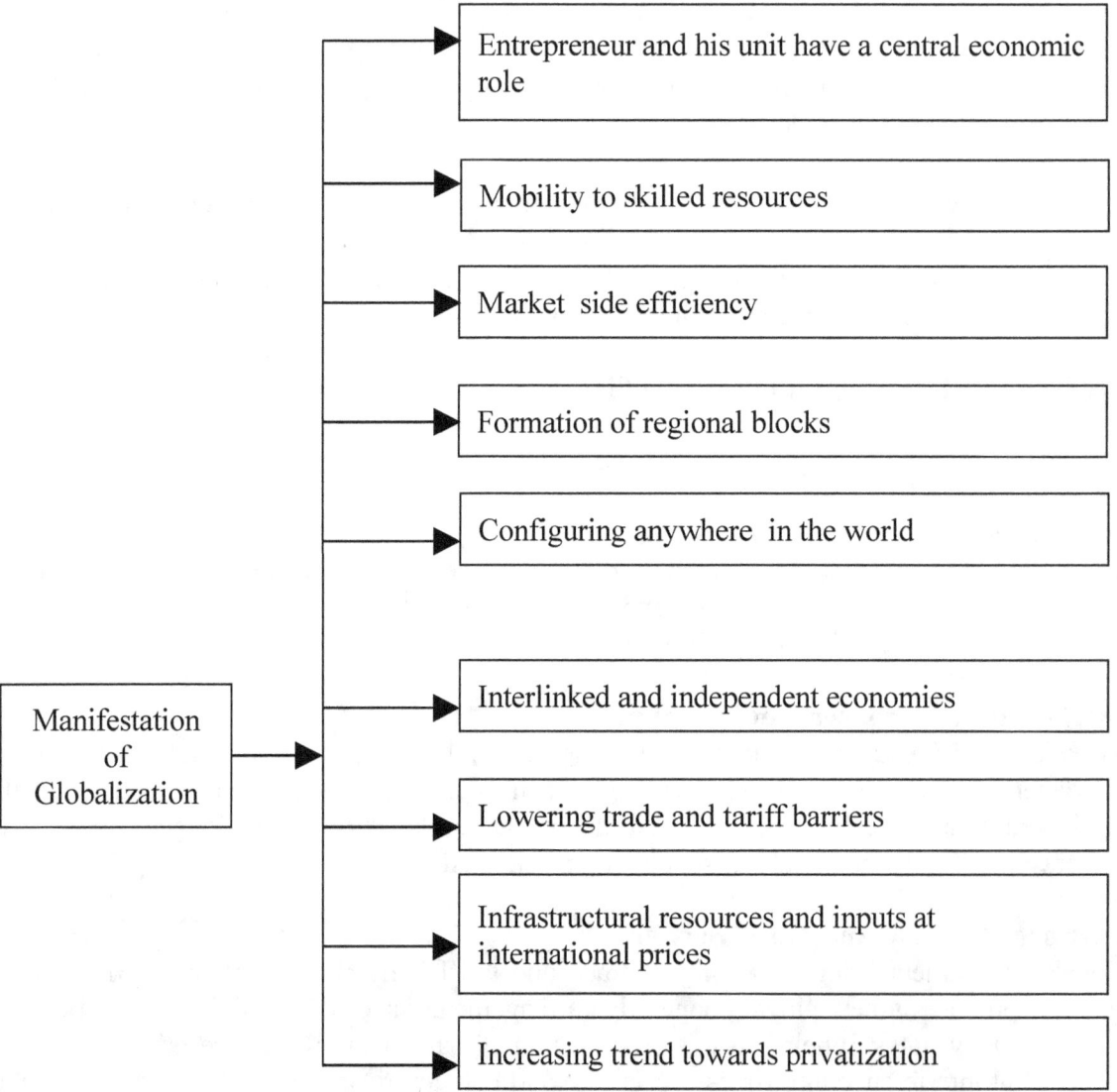

Increasing Trend Towards Privatization

In competitive scenario, governments are everywhere divesting its investment and running of the business enterprises. Government gives special importance to private entrepreneurs for greater access and freedom to run and start business units in the state. Now days, the government role is reduced to the provider of the infrastructure for private business units and help to prosper of these business units.

Entrepreneur And His Units Have A Central Economic Role

Emerging world markets, the entrepreneur and his business units role become central figures in the process of economic growth and development of country. Entrepreneurs are responsible persons and able to innovate new products, new markets, new customers and new raw materials in this way their contribute to nation's income and wealth. He takes risk and efforts put in the businesses which are rewarded in the form of profits. This is ensure to viability of the business unit. Quality and cost effective oriented firms are survived and prosper . Improper and weak firms die i.e. closedown the business units due to loss.

Mobility Of Skilled Resource

Skilled resources is also one of the important manifest of the globalization. It refers to experience, trained and educated labor in the company. Skilled labors are highly mobile from one place to another location in the world with freely mobile.

In the case , labors are unskilled that time management will be spent some money for training and education of their employees in this way enhances the skills of the unskilled labor. Factors of production like land and capital also mobile. In the case of developing country, it have long on land and short on capital it can invite by foreign investment and make good deficiency. Similarly , a developed country which have long on capital and short on land it can be used by developing country as a base for its business operations.

Factors of production like land , labor and capital can be mobile anywhere in the world.

Make- side efficiency

Integration of global market implies in terms of costs, quality processing time, these   terms of business become dominant competition drivers in the global market.. Customers will get a maximum choice of products and services on the basis of maximum value of money. State monopolies are unable to provide quality and value products to customers. Apart from this, consumers are searching the quality products and services from the global market.

Formation of Regional Block

A final result   of globalization is to formation of trade blocks. Formation of regional block is obvious. Major reasons for formation of regional block are outlined:

- ❖ To form strategic alliance to reduce economic and technological threats and leverage their respective comparative and competitive advantages.
- ❖ Important regional blocks are NAFTA (North American Free Trade Area), European Union, ASEAN, SAARC

South Asian Association for Regional Cooperation (SAARC) SAARC consist of seven South Asian Countries with Bangladesh, Bhutan, Maldives, Nepal , Pakistan and Srilanka and India. SAARC encourages and promotion of economic growth in the region. It also promote and develop social progress and cultural development in the region, it helps to active collaboration and mutual assistance in the form of economic , social , cultural , technical and scientific fields and strengthen of cooperation among the member states in the international forums on matters of common interest.

STRATEGIC RESPONSE TO THE ENVIRONMENT

It is very difficult to define , when business environment is commenced and when it will be ended in business. It is very difficult to determine the exactly environment response in the business. Strategic manager , very efforts to exploit the opportunity and reduce to weakness. Different strategic responses approaches to the environment are listed:

❖ Least Resistance
❖ Proceed with caution
❖ Dynamic response

Least Resistance

Few business just involves to manage and survival by the way of coping and adjusted with their dynamic external environment. These are simple and goals maintained. These are very passive behavior and are solely guided and supervise by the signals of the external environment.

Proceed With Caution

It is next level of strategic response to the environment, strategist are responsible to take an intelligent interest to adapt with the changing environment. Strategic managers in the company promptly seek and monitor changes in the environment, its analysis, impact on their own goals and activities will translated for assessment in terms of specific strategies survival , stability, and strength. These are regarded as the pervasive complexity and turbulence of the external environmental elements as prescribed with the framework of which they have to function like adaptive organic sub systems. It is an admittedly to suitable and modern strategy and wait for changes in business. And take corrective adaptive in nature.

Dynamic Response

This level is highly sophisticated level. In this level, external forces in business are efficiently and partially manageable and controllable by their actions in company. Feed system is highly dynamic and powerful system adopted in organization. These things not only recognize threats and weakness and ready to convert into their threats into opportunities in business environment. These are highly conscious and confident of their strengths and weaknesses of the their external environment constraints. Dynamic response have to generate a contingent set of alternatives course of action which are picked up in tune with the changing shape of business environment.

Shaping External Environment

❖ Shaping environment is one of the major problem of the business enterprise.
❖ It generate the powerful dominating behavior of command organizations may generate powerful countervailing pressure and forces in the real environment.
❖ It is more inclusive apart from the individual action in business enterprise.
❖ Its values and interests are much broader than internal environment of the business.
❖ Adopt a innovative and autonomous in organization.
❖ It happens with certain limitation of the company.

COMPETITIVE ENVIRONMENT

"Only firms who are able to continually build new strategic assets faster and cheaper than their competitors will earn superior returns over the long term".
C.C.Markides and P.S.Williamson

"Organization succeed in a competitive market place over the long run because they can do certain things their customers value better than can their competitors".
Robert Hayes, Gary Pisano, and Daid Vpton

* Strategy formulation is coping with the competition. This is basic requirement of the strategist in business.
* Intense competition is neither a coincidence nor bad luck to business organization.
* All type of business enterprise have competition with competitors in the market.
* Multinational company offered different product and services which are clash directly on every level of product and services offered by the similar Multinational companies.
* In a competitive environment, a business enterprise competition which spells out freedom of entry and exit in the matter and affects its price and scale of operations in market.
* Business enterprise have to consider their competitor's strategies , profits levels, products and services that are required for preparing and implementing their business plans.
* Nature and extent of competition of business , this is facing in the market and it is one of the major factors factors that are affecting the rate of growth , income distribution and consumer welfare.
* While formulating business policy , enterprises have to identify separately and concentration on the competitors who are significantly affecting the business in the market.
* Competitors are ready to satisfy the needs and requirement of the customer.

Nature and Extent of Competition

Nature and extent of competition is important to multinational companies and its customers. For better understanding , we shall know the following important questions that are relating to completion:
  a) Who are the competitors in the market?
  b) What are their product and services in the market?
  c) What are their market share?
  d) What are their financial positions?
  e) What is the cost of products and services in the market?

f) Who are the potential competitors ?

g) What are the future products and services which are offered to customers?

h) What is the target market?

Cooperation In A Competitive Environment

❖ Small number of only manufacture / sellers of a product may form association in this way achieve cooperation in a competitive environment.

Major purpose of cooperation in a competitive environment

❖ It is the association of manufacturer or sellers

❖ It is coordination and unification of trade practices and the determination of the best means of safeguard their interest in the form of individually an collectively

❖ It helpful to decide the price of the products and service for example OPEC

❖ It may be form for deciding market share, prices and profits etc.

❖ It may be witnessed in highly competitive business environment.

❖ For example , various credit card and finance companies are entering agreements the other business to launch co - branded credit cards and debit cards. This type of arrangements help in reaching greater number of customers.

Case – 1.1: Competitive Advantage Of The Satyam Edge

Satyam: The preferred IT services provider

With nearly a decade-and-a-half of experience in servicing global MNCs and Fortune 500 clients with end-to-end IT services, solutions and products, Satyam has come a long way, emerging as the preferred IT services provider for major global business corporations.

An innovative organization, Satyam has been a pioneer-of-sorts in the Indian IT industry.

Landmarks

❖ Pioneered the IT Offshore Development concept in India

❖ First established a satellite link for communicating with client sites

❖ Developed the unique RightSourcing delivery model

❖ Established India Development Centers for clients

❖ First to have acquired BVQI's ISO 9001:2000 certificate

❖ Developed eSCM model for ITES/BPO space with Carnegie Mellon University and Accenture

❖ **Satyam Infoway (Sify)** India's first Indian Private ISP; India's first Internet firm listed on the NASDAQ (NASDAQ: SIFY)

Advantage Satyam

❖ World class processes (SEI CMM® Level 5, ISO 9001: 2000, eSCM)

❖ Global presence (Operations in 45 countries across 6 continents)

❖ Long lasting customer relationships (Nearly 80 % of repeat business)

❖ Flexible engagement models (RightSourcing delivery model, IDCs, GDCs, JVs)

❖ Evolved competency and solution-based services

❖ Technology-led innovator

Source: Satyam Company Website (www. Satyam.com)

Cooperation On Account Of Family Ownership

❖ Cooperation is the primary tool for family owned business
❖ It generates automatically in business enterprise owned by a same family.
❖ Family is directly responsible for control , management and ownership of business.
❖ Family ownership group is nothing but a family and its kin and kith.
❖ Major and minor decisions made by the family ownership groups in business.
❖ It influence to managerial decisions and activities of the enterprise.
❖ It is identify the goals and needs of the family and its business operations
❖ Family members are amicable settlement their business constraints like properties and ownership issues

Non Cooperation On Account Of Family Ownership

❖ Quarrels with family members
❖ Conflict among the family members
❖ Family matters tend to distort their behavior in managing the business enterprise and also thereby damaging its functions.
❖ Succession problems.

COMPETITIVE ADVANTAGE

Competitive advantage refers to organization or companies how much benefit from the point views of cost and benefit analysis. Every organization has strategically competitive advantage for their business. For example, India's competitive advantage as listed below:

Exhibit –1.1 : Competitive Advantage India

"Companies around the world are gaining competitive advantages by using Indian software services that offer high quality, cost effectiveness, time savings, state-of-the-art technologies and above all reliability."
The World Bank funded study compared India with many other countries to analyse India's position vis-a-vis cost and quality. Its findings proved that India is the **best** positioned as a

high-quality and cost-effective country for software development. The advantages India offers are tremendous. They include:

· A virtual 12-hour time zone difference between India and USA offers cost and time savings provides the client with a virtual 24-hour office environment.

· A huge pool of English speaking and computer literate graduate workforce who can continue to cater to the growing demand of professionals for IT Enabled Services.

· India offers the ultimate quality advantage with relatively less costs. India has more than 137 ISO 9000 certified and 147 more companies are in the pipeline to be ISO certified by March 2001. As many as 32 Indian companies already have SEI-CMM certification, with six of them having reached Level 5. It must be noted that worldwide, only 12 companies have reached that level, and just six of them do not belong to India.

· India enjoys very strong brand equity in major markets, thanks to its growing and globally competitive software industry.

· Indian software companies believe in highest adherence to delivery schedules and customer satisfaction by using state-of-the-art technologies.

· E-Business and web based solutions : Indian companies offer the most cost-effective, innovative and extensive web-based solutions. They also offer varied solutions for E-commerce and E-Business applications. Hotmail, Junglee, WhoWhere are some of the examples of Indian innovativeness.

Other Global advantages

One of the unique methods used by Indian software companies to deliver competitive advantage to its clients involves using high-speed (64 kbps, 2 Mbps and above) datacom links, which in turn allow computers situated anywhere in the world to be used by programmers in India on a real-time and on-line basis.

Large Pool of Professionals

Just as the Gulf has its crude oil and South Africa in diamonds, India's natural resource in today's knowledge economy is its abundant technically skilled manpower. India has the second largest assembly of English-speaking scientific professionals in the world today, second only to the US. It also has a growing bank of 4.1 million technical workers, supplied by, among others, over 1,832 educational institutions and polytechnics, which train more than 67,785 computer software professionals every year. This includes the graduates passing out of the prestigious Indian Institute of Technology (IIT), where the quality of technical training is comparable to the best of the educational institutes in the world.

NASSCOM every year undertakes a survey to understand the manpower requirements of the industry. The study undertaken in 1999, highlighted the following facts:

· The number of software professionals employed have increased to 250,000 in 1999 compared to 2,00,000 in the preceding year. This includes software professionals in non-commercial organisation as well as software development units in user organisation.

· Almost 67% of the software professionals employed in the industry were in software development and operations, 3% in domain expertise development, 11% in marketing and relationship development, 15% in client support and 4% in other activities.

· The overall median age of the software professionals was about 26.2 years.

· 77% of software professionals in software companies were men, whereas 18% were women. However, this ratio is likely to be 65:35 (male : female) by the year 2003.

· Half of the software professionals possessed 5 years of working experience.

· There was an average of 21% rise in basic salary in 1998 over the previous year. However, rise in total compensation was supported by issuance of stock options to employees. During 1999, as many as 41 software and solutions companies announced employee stock options plans.

· In 1999, although the attrition rate was controlled at 16% (from the earlier turnover rate of 25% in 1992), but it still remained high, fuelled by 50% growth in the revenue for the software industry in 1998-99. This caused the HRD market to tighten considerably.

· Our software professionals were highly rated by their employers for their quality. Most gave an average of close to a 9 on a 10 point rating scale, with 1 being the lowest and 10 being outstanding.

· The skills in demand were in the area of business applications of software development, E-Commerce, Euro, software engineering, Java, ERP, CRM/ ERM, Interactive Integration Services, Datawarehousing, Internet, Client-Networking, BPR, OOPS, client-server, GUI, Windows, project management, quality assurance, technical writing, telecommunications, networking and RDBMS

Questions:
1. Explain the competitive advantage of India .

Source: NASSCOM

FIVE FORCE MODEL

Organization offering products and services which are close substitute for each other. Close substitute are products and service. They are satisfied the essential consumer needs and desire. The task facing strategic managers is to analyze competitive force in an industry environment in order to identify the strengths, weakness, opportunities and threats confronting an organization. Michael E.Porter, professor of the Harvard School of Business Administration has developed a framework, which is known as Five Forces Model. It appears in figure 3.2   helps to managers in their analysis of competitive force of the organization. This model focuses on five forces which shape to create competition within an industry. Five forces are as below:

❖ The risk of new entry by potential competitors
❖ Risk of entry by potential customers
❖ The degree of rivalry among established companies within an industries
❖ The bargaining power of supplier
❖ The closeness of substitute to the industry's product

Porter argues that the stronger each of these forces, the more limited is the ability of established organization to raise prices and earn greater profits.   Within Porter's Framework, a strong competitive force   regards as a threat since it depresses profits. A weak competitive force   views as on opportunity for   an organization to earn greater profits. Because of these forces beyond an organization's direct control like industry evaluation, the strength of five forces may change through time. In such circumstances, the task facing strategic managers is to recognize opportunities and threats in order to develop and to formulate appropriate strategic opportunities.

The character , mix and subtleties of competitive forces are never the same from one industry to another. Five force model is a powerful and widely used tool for systematically diagnosing the principles competitive pressures in a market and it should be assessing the strength.

Figure-1.12: The Five-Force Model

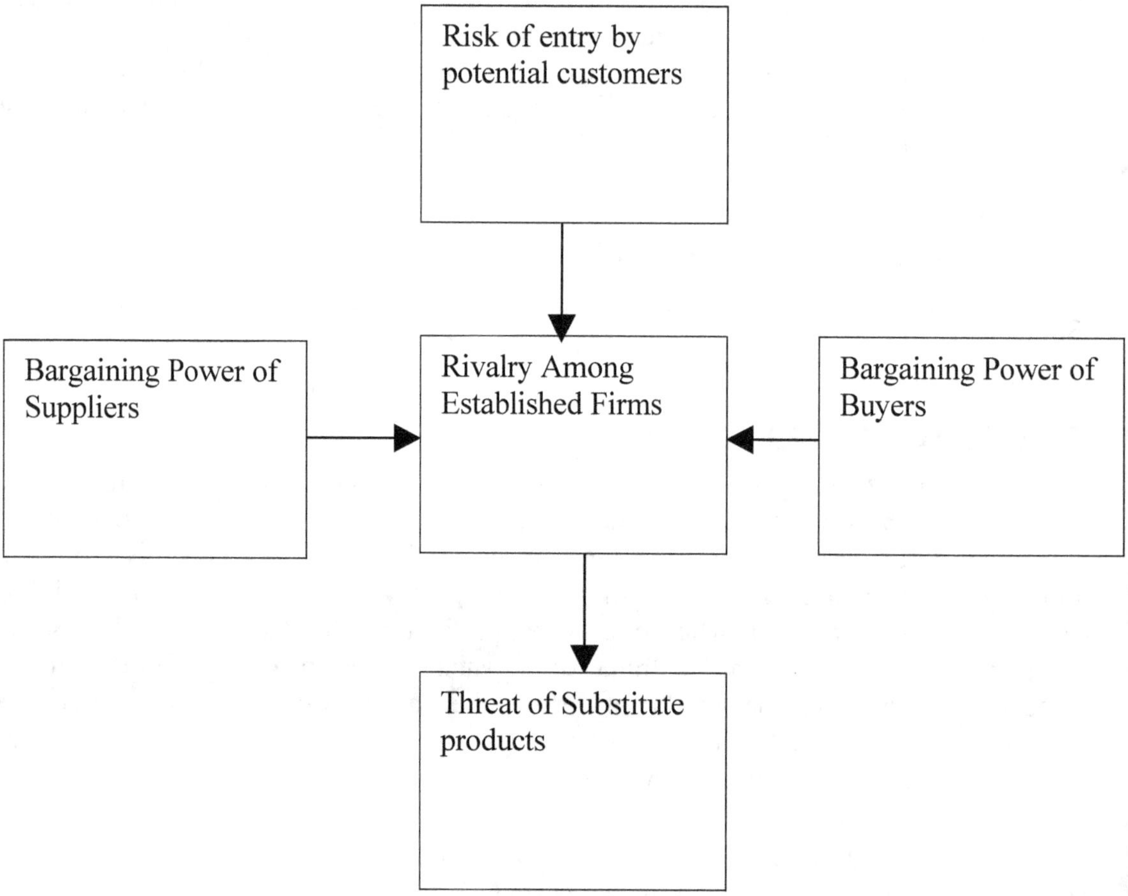

```
                        ┌─────────────────────┐
                        │ Risk of entry by    │
                        │ potential customers │
                        │                     │
                        └──────────┬──────────┘
                                   │
                                   ▼
┌────────────────────┐  ┌─────────────────────┐  ┌────────────────────┐
│ Bargaining Power of│  │ Rivalry Among       │  │ Bargaining Power of│
│ Suppliers          │─▶│ Established Firms    │◀─│ Buyers             │
│                    │  │                     │  │                    │
└────────────────────┘  └──────────┬──────────┘  └────────────────────┘
                                   │
                                   ▼
                        ┌─────────────────────┐
                        │ Threat of Substitute│
                        │ products            │
                        │                     │
                        └─────────────────────┘
```

The five force model determine competitive scenario in different industry as outlined:

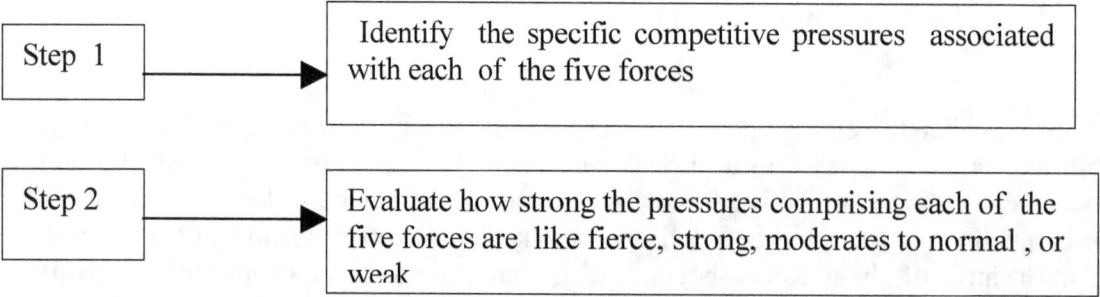

| Step 1 | → | Identify the specific competitive pressures associated with each of the five forces |

| Step 2 | → | Evaluate how strong the pressures comprising each of the five forces are like fierce, strong, moderates to normal , or weak |

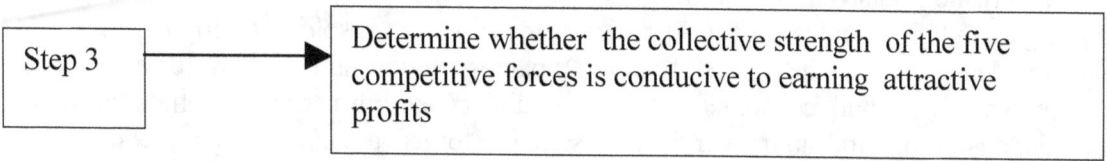

| Step 3 | → | Determine whether the collective strength of the five competitive forces is conducive to earning attractive profits |

Potential Competitors

Potential competitors are organizations which currently are not competing in an industry but they have the capability to do if they choose. Established organizations try to discourage potential competitors from entering to the industry. Since the more organizations enter an industry, it is the very difficult for the established organizations to hold there share of the market and generate to profits. Thus high risk of entry by potential competitors represents a threat to the profitability of the established organsiations. On the other hand, if the risk of new entry is low, established organizations could take advantages of this opportunity to raise prices and earn greater returns.

Economist Joe Bain who identified three main sources of barriers to new entry:

- ❖ Brand Loyalty
- ❖ Absolute cost advantage
- ❖ Economies of scale

Brand Loyalty

Brand loyalty is buyer's priority for the products of established organizations. An organization create brand loyalty through continuous advertising of brand and organizations names, patents protection of products, products innovation through organization research and development programmes, an emphasis on high product quality and providing goods after sales service. Significant brand loyalty makes it difficult for new entrants to take market share away from well established organizations. Thus it reduces the threat of entry by potential competitors.

Absolute Cost Advantages

Absolute cost advantages can arises from superior production techniques. These techniques arises due to past experience, patents, hidden process; control of particular inputs required for production like labor, materials, equipment or management skills; These access to cheaper funds because exiting organization represent low risks than established organizations. If established organizations have an absolute cost advantages, than again the threat of entry decreases.

> ### Case -1.2:Cement companies adopt innovative cost-cutting measures
>
> FOR cement companies innovation may be the key to cost competitiveness. Hence, larger cement companies such as Grasim and Gujarat Ambuja are seen to be shifting to a number of innovative cost-cutting measures to enhance bottomlines.
> These include bypassing the dealers to sell cement directly to the customer, shifting from the traditional rail-road option to cheaper sea transportation to target distant markets and

even using crushed sugarcane for meeting fuel requirements.

According to an ICRA analysis, over 80 per cent of the cement is sold currently in India is through the dealer route. "The bigger cement companies are now shifting towards a dealer-free route to supply to bulk consumers, including builders and infrastructure companies to save on the dealer margin," an industry source said. Customers are encouraged to contact the cement companies directly with their requirements, following which the manufacturer delivers the requisite quantity of cement to their doorsteps. The move also gives the companies better price competitiveness as compared to those servicing customers through the dealer route, industry players said.

Bigger players are also saving on logistics expenses, which is one of the major operating costs faced by the industry. Companies such as Gujarat Ambuja are extensively relying on the coastal transportation route to service the southern market, rather than on rail or road, according to industry analysts. Several cement companies are also using high capacity Volvo trucks for road transportation to cut down on costs, industry sources said.

In order to bring down energy costs, most of the cement companies have already shifted entirely to captive power stations and are using a variety of fuels, including pet coke and lignite. Gujarat Ambuja, in fact, has partially replaced coal with crushed sugarcane as a fuel for its Gujarat plant, according to analysts.

Cement companies are also tracking the international polypropylene prices to strike deals with manufacturers of polypropylene bags, used as packaging material in the country, according to ICRA. The scope for saving through this route is enormous, since in India cement is almost entirely sold in 50 kg bags, as opposed to it being sold in bulk in most other countries. Some of the domestic cement companies are also reportedly considering the bulk-sale route to optimise costs, industry sources said.

Questions:

1. Explain the Cement companies adopt innovative cost-cutting measures

Source: Business Line, dated June 29,2004

Economies of Scale

Economies of scale are the cost advantages associated with large organization size. Sources of scale economies include cost reductions gained through mass producing a standardized out put, discount on bulk purchase of raw material inputs and components parts, the spreading of fixed costs over a large volume. A new entrant faces the dilemma of either entering on a small scale and its result suffering a significant cost advantages or taking a very large risk by entering on a large scale and bearing significant capital costs. A further risk of large-scale entry results to increase the supply of the product will reduce the prices.

Rivalry Among Established Companies

It is the second of Porter's five competitive forces, it is the extent of rivalry among established organization within the industry. When this competitive force is weak, business organization have an opportunity to raise prices to earn greater profits. But if it is strong, business organization have an opportunity to reduce prices to earn fewer profits. It is significant due to price competition, including price wars, may result from the intense rivalry. Price competition limits reduce the profitability the on sales. Thus intense rivalry among established organizations within industry is largely a function of three factors are listed below:

- ❖ Industry competitive structure
- ❖ Demand conditions
- ❖ The height of exist barriers in the industry

Competitive Structure

Competitive structure refers to the numbers, size, and distribution of products and service in the organization in an industry. Different competitive structures have different implications for rivalry. Fragmented industries consist of a large number of small or medium sized organizations, none of which is in a position to dominate the industry. A consolidated industry dominates by small number of large organization or, in extreme cases, a monopoly (by just in one organization). Fragmented industries included agriculture, video-rental, health clubs, real estate and pharmaceuticals etc.

Low entry barriers and commodity-type products are hard to differentiate characterize many fragmented industries. The combinations of these characteristics tend to result in boom and bust cycles of the industry. Low entry barrier indicates whenever demand is strong and their impacts on profits are high. In this circumstance, there will be a flood of new entrants to cash in the boom.

In the case consolidated industry, the competitive action of the organization has directly affects the market share of its rivals, forcing to response from them. The result of the competitive interdependence can be dangerous to competitive spiral with rival companies. They are trying to undercut each other's prices of the products and service is pushing to industry and their profit down in this process. More typically, when price wars are threat, organization competes on nonprime factors like product quality and design characteristics. This type of competition constitutes an attempt to build brand loyalty and minimize the likelihood of a price war.

Demand Conditions

Industry demand conditions are another important determinant of the intensity of rivalry among the established organizations. Growing demand trends provides expansion and greater expansion of the production activity. When demand is growing ultimate result is a searching of entrants of customers or if existing customers are purchasing more of an industry products. When demand is growing, organization can increases revenues without taking a market share away from other companies.

Therefore, declining demand result in more competition from rivalry organization. It is very difficult to maintaining revenue and market share of the organization. Consumers are leaving marketplace or when individual consumer buying less. Therefore, declines the demand, declining demand constitutes a major threat to organization.

Exit Barriers

When industry demand is declining because of exit barriers are serious competitive threat for organization. Economic, strategic and emotional factors are treated as exit barriers. It keeps organization competing in an industry even when returns are very low. Organization can become locked into an unfavorable industry when exit barriers are high. Excess productive capacity tends to lead to intensified price competition, with companies cutting prices in an attempt to obtain the orders needed to utilize their idle capacity.

Exit barriers include the following

- ❖ Investment in plant, machinery and equipment that have no alternative uses and cannot be sold off if the organization wishes to leave the industry; it has to write-off the book value of the assets.
- ❖ High fixed cost of exists like severance pay to workers who are being made redundant
- ❖ Emotional attachments to an industry, as when a company is unwilling to exist from its original industry for sentimental reasons.
- ❖ Strategic relationships between business units. For instance, within multi-industry organization, a low return business unit may provide vital inputs for a high return business based in another industry. Thus the company maybe unwilling to exist from the low return business.
- ❖ Economic dependence on the industry, as when company is not diversified and so relies on the industry for it income.

The Bargaining Power of Buyers

It is third of Porter's five competitive forces; it is the bargaining power of buyer. Buyers can be influenced as competitive threat when they force down prices of the products and service. It means that when buyer demand is higher quality and better service which increasing operating costs of the products and service of the organization.

According to Porter's buyers are more powerful in the following situations:
The supply industry which consists of many small organizations and the buyers are few in number and large. These situations allow the buyers to dominate supply organizations.

- ❖ The buyer purchase in bulk in such situations, buyers can be bargained for price reductions of the products and service organization.
- ❖ The supply industry depends on the buyers orders, buyers can bargained for price reductions of the products and service of the organization.
- ❖ The buyer can switch orders between supply organizations at a low cost, thereby playing off organizations against each other to force down prices.
- ❖ It is economically feasible for the buyers to purchase the products and service from the several organizations at once.
- ❖ The buyer causes threat to supply their own needs through vertical integration, its impact on the price reducing of the products and service organization.

The Bargaining Power of Suppliers

The bargaining power of suppliers is the fourth of Porter's competitive force. Supplier influenced as a threat when they are capable to force up the price that organization must pay for products and service or reduced the quality of goods supplied thereby, reducing the organizational profitability.

In other words, weak supplier gives opportunity to organization to force down the prices and demand higher quality. As with the buyer, the capability of supplier to make demands on an organization depends on power relative to organization. According to Porter's suppliers are most powerful in the following cases:

❖ The product suppliers have sell substitutes and are important to organization.

❖ The organization industry is not an important to customer to the suppliers have does not depend on the organization's industry, and supplier have little incentive to reduce prices or improve quality of the products and service.

❖ The suppliers of the respective products are differentiated which is to more expensive for organization to switch from one supplier to another. In such circumstance, the organizations depend on its supplier and cannot play them off against each other.

❖ To raise prices, suppliers use can threat of vertically integrating forward into the industry and competing directly with the organization products and service.

❖ Buying organization cannot use the threat of vertically directly with the organization product and service.

❖ The buying organization can not use the threat of vertically integrating backward supplying their own needs as a means to reduce the product and service.

The Threat of Substitute Products

The fifth and final force in the Porter's model is the threat of substitute products - the product of industries that serve identical consumer needs as those of the industry being analysis

For instance, organizations in the coffee industry compete directly with those in the tea and soft drink industries. In the case of substitute products, if the price of the coffee rises too much relative to that of tea or soft drinks, than coffee drinkers will switch from coffee to those substitutes. The existence of close substitutes creates a strong competitive threat, limiting the price an organization.

www.ingramcontent.com/pod-product-compliance
Lightning Source LLC
Chambersburg PA
CBHW081304170526
45165CB00011B/3406